A CUP OF COFFEE WITH

10 OF THE TOP DIVORCE ATTORNEYS IN THE UNITED STATES

VALUABLE INSIGHTS THAT YOU SHOULD KNOW BEFORE YOU GET A DIVORCE

MARVIN L. SOLOMIANY
RANDY VAN ITTERSUM

OCT 2014

Rutherford Publishing House
PO Box 969
Ramseur, NC 27316
(336) 824-7012
www.RutherfordPublishingHouse.com

Cover photo: © Bigstockphoto / Yuriy Zhuravov

ISBN-10: 1499249136
ISBN-13: 978-1499249132

TABLE OF CONTENTS

ACKNOWLEDGEMENTS

We all want to thank our husbands and wives, fathers and mothers, and everybody who has played a role in shaping our lives and our attitudes.

To all the clients we've had the honor of working with, who shaped our understanding of the difficulty of this time for you and your families. It has been our privilege to serve each and every one of you.

INTRODUCTION

Contributing Author:

Randy Van Ittersum

Host & Founder – Business

Leader Spotlight Show

A s the host for the Business Leader Spotlight Show, I have the opportunity to interview leading experts in various fields. In todays connected society, most people turn to the internet to get the majority of their information. Unfortunately, it has become difficult to distinguish good information from bad, because everyone can share anything online, true or false. The Business Leader Spotlight Show's goal is to be a central place where you can get valuable accurate information about the topics we cover on the show. We try to accomplish this by interviewing the best of the best, standouts in their respective areas of expertise.

When we decided to publish a book on divorce, we set out to identify the legal leaders on that subject, and interview them to get their insights on the major issues relating to divorce. Unfortunately, it's impossible to get all the information one would want to know in a 20 minute interview. Today, we have over 2,000 minutes of expert advice from the best legal minds in the area of divorce.

We wanted the best of the best divorce attorneys collaborating on this book, so we asked ten of the best divorce attorneys we interviewed to share with you their insights into what you should know before you get a divorce. I personally believe that this is the most powerful and enlightening book ever written on the subject. It is not just one lawyer's insights on divorce, but ten of the top divorce attorneys in the United

States, from different regions of the country, sharing with you the fruit of their years of experience.

It is our hope that reading this book has two outcomes for you: first that you understand the process and the pitfalls that can be part of any divorce, and second, armed with this knowledge, you are able to proceed with your divorce in a way that not only allows you to achieve your goals, but to come out of your divorce with a sense that you are ready to begin a new chapter of your life. If you have children, we want you to be confident that you and your ex-spouse can nurture and care for them in a way that allows them to grow up knowing that they have two parents who love them and are willing to work together to see that they become healthy, responsible adults.

One of our authors, Katherine Miller, shared with me one of the best analogies I've heard about the divorce process. She said to imagine a ball of yarn that is made up of hundreds of different-colored strands of yarn, all tangled together. The divorce process is one of untangling and separating each strand of colored yarn until they are no longer intertwined.

Over the years you and your spouse's lives and assets become intertwined. Depending on the complexity of your family, assets, and liabilities, it can be fairly easy and straight forward to untangle your lives, or it can be very difficult, costly, and time consuming.

If you have young children in your family, you will be required to determine who has decision making rights with regards to a host of issues. These will include such things as religious education, medical treatment, and school activities.

You will also be required to determine parenting time. When does each parent get to see their children? Included in parenting time are issues such as holidays, birthdays, and any other special days of the year. Your divorce will also spell out which days each parent has the children during the month.

Your divorce will determine how much financial support each spouse is required to provide to support the children. Most states have set forth a formula that is followed by every couple getting a divorce in that state. As with most things in life, these issues are not cut and dried. There are many factors that are taken into consideration by the courts. Included throughout this book are powerful insights into divorce law and how it can impact one's divorce. Being educated about some of these issues can help smooth the path through your divorce.

You will learn that there are three processes available to you for divorce in most states:

- Mediation
- Collaboration
- Litigation

The divorce system has evolved to recognize that not every divorce is adversarial, requiring litigation. This book identifies many of the factors you must consider when choosing which process to use for your divorce. Armed with this information, you will be in a much better position to have a productive consultation with any divorce attorney that you are considering hiring.

As we compiled this book, one thing became crystal clear about the divorce lawyers included here: the amount of money they make from a divorce case is not their goal. Actually they prefer that you spend as little as possible to achieve your desired outcome. They understand that this is a highly emotional time in your life, and see their role as someone who can compassionately take you by the hand and guide you through the divorce process in a way to best achieve your goals.

Randy Van Ittersum
Host & Founder – Business Leader Spotlight Show

Marvin L. Solomiany
Managing Partner, Kessler & Solomiany LLC
Atlanta, GA

Mr. Solomiany provides representation in all areas of divorce, with an emphasis on high-income divorce cases, cases involving corporate entities, prenuptial agreements, and interstate child support and custody matters. He has represented in family law matters numerous athletes, entertainers, professionals and executives from Fortune 500 Companies. Mr. Solomiany has appeared in numerous radio and television programs to discuss family law issues and is a frequent lecturer in both state and national family law seminars.

DO YOUR RESEARCH BEFORE YOU HIRE AN ATTORNEY

If you came to me contemplating a divorce, the first thing I would tell you is that getting divorced is probably one of the most life-altering choices you will ever make in your lifetime. I would advise you to think long and hard about the journey you are about to embark upon. It is important that you take some time to educate yourself about the divorce process before you make your final decision to go forward.

To educate yourself, I recommend that you schedule an appointment with a divorce attorney and have him or her explain the process to you. This can easily be accomplished in a one-hour consultation. If you don't know a divorce attorney, then I would recommend that you try to get a referral from someone who you trust. If you can't get a referral, you can begin by evaluating divorce attorneys online. By doing a little research, you should be able to identify two or three attorneys whom you would like to interview. Be prepared to pay the attorney's hourly rate for any consultation you schedule.

For the initial consultation, you will want to be well-prepared so that you can get the most out of the meeting. Here are some important issues to discuss at your initial meeting.

Your attorney will need an idea of what has happened in your marriage that has led you or your spouse to want a divorce. Most states have a no-fault divorce statute, which means that it is not necessary to prove conduct, such as infidelity by the other spouse, for the Court to grant a divorce. Conduct, however, is germane to certain issues such as alimony, property division, and custody of your children. As such, it is important that you are able to explain the problems that have led you to consider divorce. Do not hide or misrepresent anything to your attorney. It is not in your best interest for your attorney to be caught by surprise by any allegations your spouse may allege during the divorce that you have not shared with your attorney beforehand. Do not be concerned about sharing embarrassing facts with your attorney. Any experienced divorce attorney is used to hearing such types of allegations.

You should be prepared to talk about your financial situation. Your attorney will want to know the financial history of both you and your spouse. He will want to know if you both work, the nature of your occupations, and whether one of you is a stay-at-home mom or dad. For purposes of division of marital property, he will need to know your assets and liabilities. You should arrive at the meeting with a good understanding of your financial picture and be prepared to discuss it during the consultation.

If you own a home or other real property, it's a good idea to know the fair market value of each property, and the remaining mortgages and loans on each property. If possible, it helps to know the monthly expenses relating to each property. Also, if possible, it's a good idea to bring your last three years' income tax returns to the meeting. With this information, a divorce attorney can give you a general idea of how the property might be divided, and how much child support and alimony may be considered and possibly awarded by the Court.

One problem that divorce attorneys frequently encounter is that a nonworking spouse has no idea how much her spouse earns. If your joint tax returns aren't easily accessible, you have the right to call your accountant and ask for a copy of your returns. You can ask to have them emailed to you, or better yet, you can pick them up. You will receive better advice from an attorney if he can actually look at your documents because he may see something on your return that you either forgot or didn't know anything about.

If you have children, the attorney will want to know the level of involvement by each party in the raising of your children. Between you and your spouse, who plans the play dates, the doctor's appointments, the teacher conferences, and the children's extracurricular activities? This information will help him to advise you about parenting issues after the divorce, such as custody and parenting time.

If you are a stay-at-home parent, your attorney will want to know what your plans are regarding entering the workplace. Do you have a marketable skillset, or will you need a period of time to go to school and learn a skill? He will want to know how that will affect the day-to-day care of your children.

After having gathered all this information, the attorney will share with you his thoughts about what to expect if you do decide to file for a divorce. It is important for you to understand that both you and your spouse's lives will never be the same after you divorce. If you have children, you will continue to have contact with each other for the rest of your lives. You are divorcing each other, not your children. The way you work out child custody issues is critical to making peace with your situation and moving forward with your life.

INSIGHTS INTO CHILD CUSTODY ISSUES

In most states, regarding the issue of child custody, the singular most important question is "What is in the child's best interest?" This question will apply to both "legal custody" and "physical custody". It is important that you understand the difference between these two issues when considering what is in your children's best interest

What is meant by legal custody? What legal custody means is the right to be informed about any important decisions concerning your children. The acronym that we typically use for those major decisions is H.E.R.E. representing Health, Education, Religion, and Extracurricular activities. Each of these issues is going to arise and will need to be addressed as you raise your children.

In most divorces, parents will be awarded what's called "joint legal custody." As a joint legal custodian, you have the right to discuss important issues with your former spouse and with any providers, such as doctors, psychologists, coaches, pastors, rabbis, or teachers who may be involved. As a joint legal custodian, you will be informed of any major questions as they arise and will be able to have your position heard on any of these issues before a final decision is made.

With respect to health decisions, it must be decided who has the right to determine elective procedures for the children, choose the doctor and/or dentist who's going to provide healthcare, and decide if the child should be seen by a psychologist. Usually the court will designate one party who has the final authority concerning those issues.

It is not necessary that one party be given final authority over all of these H.E.R.E. areas. Typically, the court will look at which parent is best suited to make these decisions in each of the areas of Health, Education, Religion, and Extracurricular activities.

For example, one parent may be a physician and therefore would be given final authority over any health matters. On the other hand, the other parent may have taken the lead in the child's religious training and therefore would be given final authority over the child's religious training. It's important to note that just because you have physical custody; it does not mean you will be given the right to have final decision authority over health, education, religion, or extracurricular activities. Often, the court will divide the responsibility among these four issues. One parent may have final authority over two issues and the other would have final say over the other two.

Depending on the state where you reside, there are different alternatives as to who and how final decision making authority is awarded. In Georgia, for example, the courts assign final authority to whichever parent is best suited for each issue or the parties can select a third party or an arbitrator to decide any issues which are in dispute.

In child custody, education is probably the most contested issue. In a situation where the parents are able to afford a private school, they tend to fight over which school the children will attend. Two other important issues that parents often disagree on are the potential requirement for a psychological educational evaluation to determine special needs, and a necessity for tutoring.

When it comes to religion, the issues are which religious faith the child will be raised in, and how much exposure or involvement the child will have within that religious faith. In most cases, by the time the parents get divorced, they have already decided if the child is to be raised Catholic, Jewish, or some other religious faith. However, as the child gets older, there are questions of whether the child should be baptized or not, have a Bar Mitzvah or not, and how much training there will be in preparation for a religious event, etc.

Extracurricular activities can also become a major problem, and many times the parties will have to return to court. The reason is that the decisions of one parent can have a big impact on the parenting time of the other parent. Some parents will use extracurricular activities as a way to get additional parenting time with the child. For example, if one parent enrolls the child in gymnastics every day for four hours, it is going to limit the time the other parent would have with the child after school.

Unless you want to end up back in court, I always tell parents that everything should be done within reason. It may mean that you can't enroll the child in an activity that's going to be more than a couple of hours each week, unless the other parent has agreed.

The courts will also address the issue of physical custody. Physical custody means whom the child is going to primarily live with. If the parents have joint legal custody, but the father has primary physical custody, this means that the child is going to be predominantly residing with the father, subject to the parenting time awarded to the mother. When the judge is deciding who should have physical custody, he will evaluate the respective parties' involvement in the child's life. He/She will also consider who is better able to provide for the "best interest of the child" going forward.

The courts understand that the roles of each parent after a divorce may be substantially different from the roles they played in the past. Roles do change after a divorce. A woman who was a homemaker and hasn't worked outside the home during the marriage, may now be required to get a job outside the home. This is going to limit her ability to be available for the children 24 hours a day, seven days a week. Therefore the court will consider not only your involvement with your children in the past, but what it is likely to be in the future. This must be taken into account when determining which parent will be in the best position to provide for "the best interest of the children" after the divorce.

There are times when the courts will award joint physical custody. This means that the child will spend virtually an equal amount of time with each parent. Joint physical custody can be shared on a variety of schedules. It could be scheduled for one week on, and one week off. One parent could have the kids every Monday and Tuesday night, while the other parent has Wednesday and Thursday nights, and they could alternate the weekends. There are many variations, but the most common are the examples just given.

Courts are sometimes hesitant to consider a joint physical custody arrangement because they don't want the child to go back and forth as some may consider this to promote instability. However, recent research supports the advantages of having joint physical custody. It disputes earlier research that opposed the notion that a child can thrive in two primary residences. Parenting roles have changed in the last 10 years. In today's families, both parents tend to be more equally involved with the children. In former times, the mom was typically the primary caretaker and wasn't working outside the home. Courts are beginning to adapt to this new dynamic, and provide joint physical custody more than they did 5 to 10 years ago.

If a party is asking for either primary physical custody or joint physical custody from the courts, it's important to present to the court a plan for implementing this arrangement. He or she should demonstrate how they are going to combine work and child care to provide for the best interest of the children.

Finally, issues of legal and physical custody are subject to modification following a divorce. Generally, a party seeking a change of legal and/or physical custody will have to show that there has been a change of circumstances since the entry of the Divorce Decree which renders the present legal and physical custody arrangement no longer in the children's best interests.

INSIGHTS INTO CHILD SUPPORT ISSUES

Another important issue regarding the children is "child support." Each state has its own Child Support Guidelines. Basically, the state formula will determine what the child support amount should be. There are two different calculations that are seen across the United States. Many states have a calculation that takes into account the incomes of both parties. Other states simply consider the income of the noncustodial parent. For instance, the state of Georgia considers not just the non-custodial parent's income, but rather both parties income when determining child support.

People often ask, "Does the party receiving the child support payments need to account for the way that money is being spent?" and the answer in most states is No. Child support calculations take into account all the things the child may indirectly or directly benefit from. The reality is that often child support payments are used to pay for a portion of the mortgage, a portion of the utilities, or a portion of auto expenses, rather than simply for expenses which benefit only the child.

The only time it is necessary to account for child support expenditures is when there is a request for an increase in child support payments. The court will want documentation to show that the presumptive amount of child support pursuant to the applicable state's child support guidelines is not adequate to provide for the children.

When discussing child support, people usually are referring to the direct payment that one party is making to the other. However, child support can consist of different types of payments, other than the usual direct payment to the custodial parent. For example, payment of insurance premiums for medical insurance and out-of-pocket expenses can be part of a child support obligation. Similarly, payment for a child's private school tuition and extracurricular activities can also be part of a child support obligation. In some states, the cost of life insurance can be factored into the child support obligation. The courts will consider many of these expenses beyond just the monthly payment calculation that a state may use to determine the direct child support payment to the payee.

Child support in most states will continue until the time the child has completed high school, not to exceed age 20. A minority of states will require child support to be paid until the child actually completes college.

As in custodial issues, the amount of child support can be modified following a divorce. Most states require a showing of a change of financial circumstance or a change in the needs of the child in order to modify the existing child support obligation. Typically, a child support modification actions is filed when the payor's income has either substantially increased or decreased.

INSIGHTS INTO PROPERTY DIVISION IN A DIVORCE

You will have to deal with property division in your divorce. There are two legal principles that a court will apply to determine the division of the marital estate. A state either applies the approach known as "equitable division of property" or "community property."

A majority of the states use "equitable division" of marital property. This means that the property that will be subject to division is only property that was acquired during the marriage. Premarital-acquired property is commonly referred to as separate property. In an equitable division state, the court will allow the party who brought property into the marriage to retain that property, provided that the party is able to prove that he or she brought that property into the marriage and typically that no efforts during the marriage contributed towards the increase in the value of the premarital property.

Equitable however, does not mean equal. Equitable means what is fair under the circumstances, considering the merits of each case as determined by the Court. The courts typically will start from a point where a 50-50 division of property is fair, and then will deviate as necessary from that 50-50 division. The court can give a majority of the property to one spouse, or it can divide the property any way it deems appropriate, for example 60% - 40%, 70% - 30%. It does not have to divide the property 50-50.

The court has a lot of latitude to determine what is equitable in each case. The court will consider the conduct of the parties leading up to the divorce. They will factor in who has a greater ability to recover the assets that he or she is going to be giving up in the divorce. The court can look at the length of the marriage, the age of the parties, and the health of each party. If either party has a lot of separate

14

property, that may also influence the court's decision about division of the marital property.

Another very important consideration is the contributions that both spouses may have made to acquire the marital property, or to maintain the family unit during the marriage. The court will look at who contributed financially towards the acquisition of assets, and also what involvement the other party may have had towards maintaining the family unit. There are also situations where one party was not involved in the acquisition of the assets, but because that party was able to stay at home and allow the other party to go out and develop his or her professional reputation, the family unit was able to acquire the assets.

Some states use the second approach which is commonly referred to as the "community property system." The major difference between a community property state and an equitable division state is that in a community property state the judge has no discretion when it comes to dividing marital assets. Once the judge determines that an asset is community property, the court has to divide the estate equally between the parties.

INSIGHTS INTO ALIMONY IN A DIVORCE

The courts will also determine if alimony should be paid to one of the parties. Alimony is probably one of the most hotly-contested issues in a divorce case. The two main issues regarding the determination of alimony relate to the amount and duration of the alimony.

In most states, and unlike child support, a spouse is not automatically entitled to alimony. The need for alimony must be proven by the person seeking the alimony. The court will require a financial affidavit from the person requesting alimony, including a budget that demonstrates that the person will not be able to meet his/her reasonable expenses without receiving alimony.

Some states have alimony guidelines which enumerate not only the factors that a court is to consider, but perhaps most importantly, the range of alimony to be awarded by the courts. Nonetheless, the majority of states do not have alimony guidelines that require a Judge to order a specific amount and duration of alimony. In such states, typically there are two primary factors that the court will consider when determining whether you should receive or pay alimony. These are the payor's ability to pay alimony, and the payee's need for that alimony. However, depending on a state's guidelines, additional factors can be taken into consideration. Many states have adopted a form of the Uniform Marriage and Divorce Act which states that alimony shall be in amounts and for periods of time the court deems just after a consideration of all relevant factors. Such factors, include, but are not limited to, the following: (a) financial resources of both parties; (b) ability of the party seeking alimony to obtain education/meaningful employment; (c) standard of living established during the marriage; (d) duration of the marriage; (e) age and emotional condition of the spouse seeking alimony; (f) ability of spouse paying alimony to simultaneously meet the needs of both spouses; and (g) fault.

Although all of these factors are important, the most common reason to receive alimony is to give a party enough time to become self-supporting. In other words, how many years does one need to be supported before one is able to go out and support oneself?

Someone who gets divorced later in life may have less ability to earn a living than someone getting divorced in their mid-20s or in your late 30s. Under this situation, the court could very well provide that alimony be paid for as long as the payer is working. On occasion, especially in those circumstances where the person receiving the alimony is ill, they may receive alimony for his/her life.

The court will also consider the ability of the spouse paying alimony to meet his or her own financial obligations after alimony payments.

In some states a person's infidelity can affect his or her right to receive alimony. If the party seeking alimony has been unfaithful, and that infidelity was the reason for the divorce, the court may bar that person from receiving alimony.

Some states also will consider whether that infidelity was forgiven or condoned after it took place. In those states, if the injured party became aware of the infidelity and continued to live as husband/wife with his/her spouse, the past infidelity may not be a bar to alimony.

You should always tell your attorney the truth about any possible conduct issues which may be relevant to your divorce. I always tell clients that in most instances "the lie is worse than the crime." The worst thing a client can do is to lie about a conduct issue and then get caught with that lie. Once a court determines that a person has not been truthful about his/her testimony, the court will be inclined to believe that they have also been lying about other matters relating to the divorce case.

There are two types of alimony: periodic alimony and lump sum alimony. Periodic alimony is paid monthly until a specific date. For example, alimony payments might be $2,000 a month for 24 months or until the person receiving alimony remarries. Also, alimony may terminate if you are living a meretricious relationship (meaning that you are continuously living with someone who is contributing towards your expenses and your needs).

Periodic alimony is tax-deductible for the payor and taxable to the recipient. For example, if one receives $36,000 a year of alimony, that will be taxed by the federal government just as if the amount were earned.

By contrast, lump sum alimony is specific as to the number of payments and the amount of each payment. It does not necessarily mean that you're going to pay a single lump sum payment. Unlike periodic alimony, which terminates upon a given event, lump sum alimony terminates only when you have paid the total amount of money that you have agreed to pay. Lump sum alimony is not tax deductible to the payor or counted as income to the payee.

CAN I MODIFY PROVISIONS IN MY DIVORCE AFTER IT HAS BEEN SETTLED?

Certain provisions in a divorce can be modified after the final divorce decree. Other provisions cannot be modified, such as property division. Provisions relating to custody and parenting time are modifiable. Likewise, child support and alimony obligations can be modified if you are able to meet the burden of proof required by the Courts.

An involuntary reduction in your income can justify a modification in either child support or alimony payments. For example, if you formerly had an income of $200,000, and your job was terminated, then you would have the right to go back to court and ask for a modification. Typically, a 15% reduction in your income is sufficient to get you into court, but there is no guarantee that the court will modify your payments. A modification case is a two-step process. The first step is to show that your income and/or financial situation has detrimentally changed since the divorce. Once you have proven that, you will have to prove that based on this change, you are no longer able to meet the previously-specified amount of child support or alimony payments. However, if you have substantial assets that can be used to pay child support even though you may be unemployed or have experienced a reduction in income, the court is not required to reduce your obligations, as you may still have the financial ability to pay the alimony/child support.

A mistake people make often in these situations is to think that that because you're no longer earning your previous income, your obligation is reduced automatically from the time you experienced the reduction in income. Nothing could be further from the truth. To reduce any court ordered payments like alimony and child support, you will first have to initiate a legal action which will result in a new order being issued by the courts. Until that order is issued, your obligation remains the same, pursuant to the last support order.

You should be aware that during the time you're seeking a modification, if you don't pay the required amounts, you can be held in contempt of court, a charge that carries stiff punishment. You can be jailed or you can be ordered to pay not only the actual amounts previously ordered by the Court, but also interest and attorney's fees.

INSIGHTS ON PRENUPTIAL AGREEMENTS

Most states allow you to enter into a prenuptial agreement. A prenuptial agreement is like getting divorced before you ever get married. The primary purpose of a prenuptial agreement (also known as "antenuptial agreements") is to determine what would happen if the parties eventually obtained a divorce. These agreements address many financial issues such as alimony and property division. Typically, they do not cover issues like child support and child custody, as issues solely relating to the children are ultimately for the Court to decide at the time of an actual divorce.

The decision to enter into a prenuptial agreement is obviously a very personal decision, that is heavily influenced by the number of assets that you're bringing into the marriage, and the income that you may be earning at the time of your marriage. It is not unusual for people who have been divorced before to want a prenuptial agreement because of their experience with their previous divorce.

There are three main issues to consider in a prenuptial agreement: identification of separate property, identification of marital property, and alimony.

The first step is designating which property will be considered separate property. Typically, and absent a prenuptial agreement, states recognize separate property as that property you bring into the marriage or inherit during the marriage. However, in a prenuptial agreement, there are no limitations as to what can be considered separate property. For example, it can include earnings during the marriage, any assets that you acquire from your earnings, or any assets that you acquire from the reinvestment of property you brought into the marriage.

The next issue is marital property. In a prenuptial agreement, you will define which property will be divided in the event of a divorce, and how it will be divided. You can specify whether it will be divided equally between the spouses, or whether it will be divided by some other percentage that you and your soon-to-be spouse agree upon.

Finally, a prenuptial agreement can have specific provisions regarding alimony. Some prenuptial agreements state that there will be a complete bar to alimony in the event of a divorce. Other prenuptial agreements will provide for a specific schedule of alimony payments, which can be either periodic alimony payments or lump sum alimony awards.

The main point of a prenuptial agreement is to prevent any uncertainty about what will happen in the event of a divorce. People entering into a prenuptial agreement know exactly, as of the date they sign the agreement, what they are going to be entitled to in the event of a divorce.

Generally, prenuptial agreements are enforceable throughout the United States, but the courts will look at different factors to determine whether the Prenuptial Agreement is valid at the time of the divorce. Typically, they will look at whether that agreement was obtained through fraud, or misrepresentations of material facts. The most important issue is to make sure that there had been a full, fair and detailed financial disclosure by both parties when the agreement was signed. In most situations, court will require that such financial disclosure be part of the actual prenuptial agreement, so there are usually exhibits attached to the prenuptial agreement for each parties' financial disclosure/statement.

The second factor the court will consider is whether the agreement was unconscionable. Unconscionability is a legal term often defined as "entering into a contract that no person would otherwise enter into." It's very difficult to prove that an agreement was unconscionable at the time it was signed. Unconscionability is not the same as fair. Typically, most prenuptial agreements are unfair by their very nature.

The third factor the court will consider is whether the facts and circumstances have changed since the date of the marriage, so as to render the agreement unfair at the time of its enforcement. Since there are always unforeseen circumstances that arise in marriages, typically such change of circumstances will be limited to some extravagant event such as a change in a person's health that renders that person disabled or simply unable to support him/herself. Infidelity, children, or change in financial circumstances will not be considered by the court as unforeseen.

INTER-STATE CUSTODY, VISITATION AND CHILD SUPPORT

More than ever, we are seeing an increase in child custody and child support disputes when parents reside in different states. We also continue to see a trend of parents wanting to relocate to a different state from the one where they were married or divorced.

There are myriad reasons for one of the divorced parties wanting to relocate to a different area of the state or even move to a different state. It is important to understand that prior to any relocation, you need to provide notice to the other parent, and in most states, may have to seek permission from the court to move.

When relocation requests are made, the court will want to know the reason that you want to relocate. You can't just say that you want to move, you must have an important reason for wanting to do so. Regardless of the reason, the court will be bound to make a decision that is in the child's best interest. Within this determination, the court will not only look at the reason for the relocation, but also will examine the potential impact the relocation would have on the children's relationship with the parent who remains in the state, and what effect, if any, a relocation would have on child support obligations and on parenting time. While the court can't prevent a parent from moving, the court certainly can prevent a child moving with that parent. In addition, in a relocation case, the court will most likely modify child custody, child support, and parenting time to protect the spouse who remains behind.

These cases are typically hotly-litigated because a parent's relationship with the children will be significantly affected if the other parent moves with the children. The parent who remains in the state will not be able to see the children in their extracurricular activities or in religious or school functions. He or she will be missing out on significantly more than just a portion of their parenting time.

If you want to modify child support or child custody, and you live in different states, you have to figure out which state has jurisdiction. If a party or a child continues to reside in the state that issued the last support order, then you have to pursue the modification action in that state. For example, if the parties are divorced in Georgia, and following the divorce Mom and the children move to the State of Alabama, and Mom wants to get an increase in child support, she will have to file that action in the state of Georgia, since one of the parties continues to reside in the state.

Continuing the same example, let's say that the mom moved with the kids to Alabama, and she has been in Alabama for a couple of years, and now the father wants to modify his parenting time. Father has to file his case in the State of Georgia as Georgia continues to have exclusive continuing jurisdiction (since one of the parties continues to reside in the state following the divorce). The State of Georgia will then determine whether it wants to retain jurisdiction of that action, or whether it wants to transfer the case to the State of Alabama because it may find that it is a more convenient forum. The initial action always has to be in the state that issued that last order, provided that a parent or a child continues to reside in that state.

If you are contemplating getting divorced, I hope that this chapter allows you to enter into that decision with your eyes wide open. As I pointed out in the beginning, it is probably one of the most life-altering choices you will ever make. I hope that I have provided you with valuable insights about the divorce process, so that you are prepared before you decide to go forward with a divorce.

(This content should be used for informational purposes only. It does not create an attorney-client relationship with any reader and should not be construed as legal advice. If you need legal advice, please contact an attorney in your community who can assess the specifics of your situation.)

Daisy Benavidez
Grand Rapids Law Group PLLC
Grand Rapids, MI

Daisy Benavidez is one of the founding partners of the law firm Grand Rapids Law Group PLLC and is an experienced litigator, negotiator and advocate on behalf or her clients. She is dedicated to protecting her client's rights and helping them navigate the complicated world of divorce and family law. Practicing law is more than a job for her. She loves having the privilege of being able to help others through some of the most difficult times of their lives.

TWELVE FACTORS IN CHILD CUSTODY

If I were having a cup of coffee with a friend and she shared with me the fact that she was thinking about getting a divorce, I'd give her the following advice. First, I'd ask what her ultimate goal is, what would make her the happiest, and what she could settle for. There are very few divorces that are uncontested. If it's going to be a contested divorce, the number one priority should be to find the right divorce attorney for the case. I recommend interviewing several divorce attorneys until the right one for the job is found. You want to find an attorney who you feel comfortable with because your attorney is going to be somebody who not only fights for you, but who becomes your shoulder to cry on. Divorce is probably the toughest thing that person will ever have to live through.

Divorce is not fun for the people involved. The person once considered one's best friend and true love is now one's heartbreak and opponent. You marry your best friend, and then, all of a sudden, you hate each other. You're enemies. Once there are kids involved, it can be even messier if one parent's ultimate goal is to make the other's life miserable rather than the putting the child's best interest first. It is always smart to remember the children love both parents, and they have a right to love, affection, and relationships with both parents. Therefore, the parents will end the marriage through the divorce; however, they will continue to see each other and interact because they will share the happy and sad moments of their child's life. Dealing with an ex-spouse doesn't stop when a child graduates from high school. One will still deal with an ex-spouse when a child graduates from college. One will still deal with an ex-spouse when the grandchildren are born. That's why it's very important that you interview different attorneys and see whom you feel comfortable with so that everything is done to your satisfaction from the beginning.

An entire history of the marriage is needed to be efficient and thorough in any divorce case. History will include information about marital property, debts, and separate property. This information is very important for a property settlement or trial. If children are involved, then information about the children, living arrangements, roles of each parent, and what is in the child's best interest is crucial information to obtain at the start of a divorce.

GROUNDS FOR A DIVORCE IN MICHIGAN

Michigan is a no-fault divorce state. That means that all the plaintiff (the person who files a divorce) has to state is that there has been a breakdown in the marital relationship to the extent that the objects of matrimony have been destroyed, and there remains no reasonable likelihood that the marriage can be preserved. No other statement of grounds is permitted in the complaint, so you can't start throwing blame, like we need a divorce because this person committed adultery. One can throw mud later if there is a trial over the marital estate distribution, but that's the only time blame would actually come into consideration. Even then, the courts are very careful when it comes to fault. In Michigan, the only allegation that can be made is what the statute states: "that there has been a breakdown of the marriage relationship to the extent that the objects of matrimony have been destroyed and there remains no reasonable likelihood that the marriage can be preserved."

DOMESTIC VIOLENCE

Some people involved in divorce allege domestic violence, whether it does or doesn't occur in the relationship, to gain an advantage. A true victim of domestic violence should always file a police report. Always request a no contact order or personal protection order. Domestic violence should be reported, and the aggressors should be prosecuted.

Once a person alleges domestic violence, regardless of whether there are police reports filed or not or whether the client was convicted or not, it gives the complainant an advantage if the court believes that it occurred. Victims of domestic violence sometimes gain access to a free attorney, which is great because here in Michigan, courts do not appoint divorce attorneys. This is a great benefit because it saves complainants thousands of dollars. Divorces are pricey, and divorce attorneys usually require a large retainer upfront, then bill on an hourly basis.

Another advantage is gained for victims of domestic violence when they obtain a personal protection order. Many times, on the advice of their attorney, a victim immediately runs down to the court and files a personal protection order, which will keep the other party away from them and their children.

If the allegation is that the opposing spouse is a violent person, the victim automatically has the upper hand on custody and the upper hand on remaining in the marital home while the divorce is pending. If the victim is granted custody or more parenting time than their spouse, they are normally granted the benefits of child support and remaining with the children in the home. The victim has the opportunity to request supervised parenting time for the opposing spouse. Supervised parenting time can be held at centers at a cost to the parent who gets supervised parenting time. A parent whose parenting time must be supervised under court order will sometimes have to pay between $50-100 just to spend that hour or two with their children because the other side is claiming domestic violence. Domestic violence is one of the factors that Michigan looks at when evaluating custody and parenting time.

In a divorce case in which domestic violence exists, three cases may be open at the same time. There'd be a criminal case, a personal protection order case, and a divorce case.

RESPONDING ON A TIMELY BASIS

The defendant, the person who did not file the divorce, will need to be served with a summons and complaint for divorce once it has been filed. Once a person is served, they are required to submit an answer to the complaint no later than 21 days if personally served, or 28 days if served by mail.

It is crucial to meet these deadlines. If an answer isn't filed by the 21 or 28 days, a default is entered, and the opportunity to respond is gone. Courts allow an answer to be filed after the deadline, but only for reasons outlined in the Michigan Court Rules.

The personal protection order is the quasi type of case. It's a quasi-criminal, quasi-domestic case. It has criminal overtones, since you will be sent to jail if you come near that person, so your liberty is at risk if you do not obey the order. But it's domestic because it's done in a civil court. Personal protection orders, or PPOs, are separate cases from the divorce, and they would be filed with a different case number. However, here in Michigan, at least in Kent County, the judge for your divorce is the same judge that you'd have for the PPO.

A spouse can file a PPO because they're victims of domestic violence, and they want the other party kept away, and they're afraid of what the "aggressor" spouse is going to do once a divorce is filed. After the respondent has been personally served with a PPO, he or she has 14 days to respond to the allegations in the PPO, to request a modification or that the court rescinds the PPO.

THE COSTS IN A DIVORCE CASE CAN BE HANDLED IN A VARIETY OF WAYS

Everyone wants to know, "Who pays attorney fees in a divorce?" The answer is that it depends on the situation. The most popular scenario is that each party hires their own attorney, and both are responsible for their own legal fees. In my opinion, this is the best way to handle parties' attorney fees because both parties are going to play nicer if it's costing them money out of their own pockets to drag out a case or be difficult and unreasonable for the wrong reasons.

Other options include an order or agreement that one spouse will pay all attorney fees, or working with agencies that provide pro bono attorney representation to people who qualify.

MEDIATION AS AN ALTERNATIVE TO LITIGATING THE DIVORCE

Some Michigan courts require mediation. Depending on the parties' willingness and desire to settle, attorneys would be able to help parties determine whether mediation, arbitration, or other alternative dispute resolution options are preferable for the case. In some counties where mediation is required, parties can only be excused from it if there are allegations of domestic violence, personal protection orders involving the parties, or if the parties have already settled.

Mediation is a great option if the parties have the right attitudes. Mediation helps get the case settled without having to put all the responsibility on the judge. Mediation will allow the parties to have a better result, a result they're both going to be able to live with from the start. Mediation is a better option to resolve a divorce case than having a trial. In a trial, a case isn't necessarily over once the trial is complete because one can always appeal the judgment. In mediation, both sides have an input in the resolution, and it is a less intimidating process than a trial. A neutral party listens to both sides and helps craft an arrangement that'll work for both, and hopefully both sides are happy in the end. After mediation, you're not going to walk out of there and say, "Oh, yeah! I am the champion!" instead you'll say something like, "I can live with this. Glad it is over without having to go to trial." The post-judgment appeals problems are eliminated, and money is kept in the parties' pockets instead of the appellate attorneys' pockets.

DETERMINING CHILD CUSTODY IS A COMPLEX ISSUE IN DIVORCE CASES

When it comes to custody and to parenting time, the spouses seldom agree in a contested divorce. This is a point of much contention during divorces. When it comes to custody, I always ask my clients, "What is the arrangement now? Are the children happy? What is the best scenario for the children? What is it that you want? What would you settle for? What would you be happy with? What could you live with?" And we go from there.

If child custody is a contested issue, then there are several different things that can happen. Part of the case can be sent to a mediator, or be sent over to Friend of the Court for a resolution or evaluation and recommendation to the court so the judge can make an informed decision.

An evaluator from Friend of the Court sits down with both parties at the same time and interviews them. After the interview, a report and recommendation are prepared for the judge. The report usually details case facts for every factor that the law requires the courts to consider in order to decide the custody and parenting time that would be in the children's best interest. That recommendation will include who the children should be with, or what custody arrangement is in the best interest of the children. A party can still object to the recommendation of the Friend of the Court evaluator. A timely objection will prevent the recommendation from becoming a final order. Once one's objections are made, the court will conduct an evidentiary hearing on the objection or address this at trial. How much weight a Friend of the Court's report is given varies by judge, by referee, and by the Friend of the Court evaluator. This report and recommendation are just additional things that the court weighs.

Mediation will assist both parties in reaching an agreement regarding child custody or parenting time. The end result of mediation would be an agreement between the parties, and that would not be contested.

The best interest of the child is the standard here in Michigan for determining custody. There are 12 individual factors that the judge looks at one by one to determine the best interest of children.

Two types of custody exist here in Michigan. One is physical, and the other is legal. Legal custody really means that both parents have a say, and both parents can decide on the important decisions of upbringing, education, religion, and medical care. Michigan courts usually encourage reaching joint decisions with respect to legal custody, unless you can convince the court that the parents cannot communicate, that they cannot agree on important issues involving the children, and that it would have a negative impact on the children for them to share legal custody. The downside of that is that once a parent has sole legal custody, then the parent can move anywhere they want. The court would have to let the parent go.

If both parties have joint legal custody, they both have a say in important issues. If there is a disagreement about a specific area and parents cannot agree, then the final decision will be made by the judge.

JUST TWO WORDS

The courts are trying to stay away from the words "physical custody." Parties will avoid settling a case and litigating case because they don't want the final judgment of divorce to say that the other side has "physical custody." We are seeing a trend of the courts taking that phrase, "physical custody," out of the judgments and replacing it with "parenting time."

Physical custody is be defined as having the child 50 percent or more of the time. In a case where both parents share nearly equal amounts of time, one parent shouldn't have sole "physical custody." A cleaner, more neutral way to keep both sides happy would be to grant both parents "parenting time" and then set up a schedule. Really, physical custody just means the number of days that the children stay with the other parent, so it's still parenting time. "Physical custody," those two words, have really clogged up the system.

Most judges want parents to have equal parenting time unless it's not in the best interest of the children. Michigan law states that it will be in the best interest of children for both parents to be involved in a child's life.

FIRST RIGHT OF REFUSAL

The first right of refusal is a provision that can apply to some divorces in Michigan. Under the first right of refusal, a parent who is unable to have the children during their designated parenting time and needs a caretaker for that time will first have to give the other parent the option of having that parenting time with the children.

The first right of refusal does happen in Michigan, but it's not mandatory. The parties have to agree to that, or you have to present a very good case to the judge as to why that's in the best interest of the children. Depending on their relationship, and the reason for the request, I encourage my clients to cooperate. You can look at this way: the children get more time with the other parent, and who is better qualified to care for the children than their own parent? Plus, it's free babysitting! A divorce is very difficult for everybody involved, especially the children. First right of refusal is a great thing for everyone if done for the right reasons. It makes relationships stronger. I would not recommend first right of refusal if the other parent isn't a good parent, but in most cases, they are.

THE TWELVE BEST INTEREST FACTORS IN CHILD CUSTODY

Twelve factors are considered in assignment of custody in Michigan. The court might decide that some of the factors in a case are more important than others; however, the court must consider and make a decision about each factor. The court will also look at the whole picture to decide what custody and parenting time arrangements are in the best interests of your child.

The first factor is the love, affection, and other emotional ties existing between the parties involved and the child. Most of the time, the court will find that both parents love and have affection for the child, and both have emotional ties. However, they might find that somebody has closer parental emotional ties because, for example, a wife may have given birth, and it's natural birth. She nursed the child. Maybe Dad was absent the entire time, so the mother's really the one who came and provided the medical and dental care. She's been more involved in their education. The children are very clingy to the mother or the other parent. So if the kids want to be with that parent the entire time, then obviously, that shifts the weight a little bit more towards the mother when you can see those strong emotional ties. Usually this factor is given to both parents because both parents love their children.

The second factor is the capacity and the disposition of the parties involved to give the child love, affection, and guidance and to continue the education and raising of the child in his or her religion or creed, if there is any. It almost sounds the same, but this is actually continuing the status quo, not making huge changes. A divorce is already something very traumatic for children, and it is a huge change. The court has to discern which parent has the desire and disposition and capacity to continue that guidance and to continue raising them in their religion and their education. This factor can be advantageous to the parent who was the primary caregiver, if the other parent was largely absent. It really comes down to a case by case basis. The judge will look at that family. Who do the children go to? The history plays a big role when evaluating most of these factors. It's not just a matter of the mom giving birth, so therefore, she wins on this factor. It's not like that at all. You look at every single detail of that family's life history and the relationship with the children.

The third factor is the capacity and the disposition of the parties involved to provide the child with food, clothing, medical care, and other remedial care recognized and permitted under the laws of Michigan. Courts might find that both parties have the capacity and disposition to provide the children with food, clothing, and medical care.

The fourth factor is the length of time that the child has lived in a stable, satisfactory environment and the desirability of maintaining that continuity. The age of the child, the physical environment, and the inclinations of the custodian and the child regarding the permanency of the relationship, also need to be considered in child custody. It can also be defined as a custodial relationship of significant duration, which means the child has been living with this certain person, and this person has actually been the one who has provided this child with parental care, discipline, love, guidance, and attention appropriate to the age of the child and his or her individual needs. Every family is different, and every child is different. The courts look at the environment in both the physical and psychological senses, in which the relationship between the custodian and the child is secure, stable, and permanent. I think this is one of the most important factors. The custodial environment of a child is a very important term in family law because the judge will always consider that when making any changes to custody. Even if there's a motion to change custody or parenting time later on, the court does not like to disrupt that custodial environment. The way Michigan law defines this is that the custodial environment of a child is where, over an appreciable time, the child naturally looks to the custodian in that environment for guidance, discipline, and the necessities of life and parental comfort. It can be with one parent, both, another person, or it could be with neither. Courts don't like to disrupt the custodial environment of the child; it is the standard of proof in making any changes or custody determinations. Courts want to maintain that continuity and stability.

The fifth factor is the permanence, as a family unit, of the existing or proposed custodial environment or home. The judge will look at both parents who are fighting for physical custody. The judge will look at, for instance, Mom's custodial home right now. What's her house like? Who all is living in it? Is it a family, or is she with a bunch of roommates, with guys coming in and out? How permanent is it? Maybe she's been moving from place to place for the past six months, taking the kids out of school, with different people coming in and out their homes and lives. On the other hand, maybe the father gets a girlfriend right away, but this is actually somebody he's been living with since right before one of them actually filed for a divorce, and he's already proposed to her. The court may believe there's more permanence there. There's going to be a family in that home. So if that were the case, the father would win on this factor. There has to be a stable and satisfactory home, a suitable home for the children.

The sixth factor is the moral fitness of the parties involved. This factor can be entertaining or annoying for the courts and attorneys at times, depending on their personalities, because this is where everybody's dirty laundry is aired. Things can get pretty nasty. Once the mudslinging begins, I always have to remind my client, "How did that piece of dirty laundry affect the child? Did that have an impact on the child?" An example of a common piece of dirty laundry, or mud if you like that metaphor better, is adultery. People think, "Well, you know, I'm going to get custody because my wife was having an affair. She had at least two affairs, and it's been going on our entire marriage." But the question is, did that ever affect her being a good mother? It doesn't automatically preclude her from getting custody of her minor children because she maybe has been a good mother. She has performed most of the day to day responsibilities of feeding, clothing, educating, and providing medical care for the kids. Some people are freaked out if they've been unfaithful; they think they're going to lose custody. The opposite side of that coin is a husband who is unfaithful but still a great father, married to a mother who is never home, who forgets to pick up the kids, and who never takes the kids to the doctor's. Maybe the father who's having an affair with the nurse is the primary caregiver whose top priorities are the well-being of the children and taking over the major responsibilities of feeding, clothing, and providing medical care. Sometimes a party will bring up that the other party (for example, the mom) was living with another man before being married, and that's immoral. He seems to think that because she wasn't married to him, that makes her promiscuous. Well, her previous history doesn't really matter. The facts that the court considers under this factor have to comply with what the Child Custody Act intended to do. It has to be in the best interest of the children. The "immoral" behavior must be proven to have affected the children in a negative way emotionally or physically. Another fun topic is the woman's moral fitness from before she ever had children. Again, how does that affect the kids now? Every case is unique.

The seventh factor is the mental and physical health of the parties involved. If there's a chronic illness or a mental illness that's actually going to affect the child, then the court looks at that and makes a decision as to how much weight they're going to give that factor.

The eighth factor is that the court will look at the home, school, and the community record of a child. If the children have a good home, school, and community record at the marital home, and the mother plans to keep the marital home, and she's winning on all these other factors, then she'll probably also win on the eighth factor because this is where the children have lived for so long. The court will consider all the factors, give each factor what it deems appropriate weight, and also look at the big picture. For instance, let's say the kids have lived in this home their entire lives. One of the parents is keeping the home, but they're both good parents. The court, in this specific case, wants to try and award joint custody because they're both good parents for the children. The children want to be with both of them. If the children can adapt to new situations, as evidenced by family travels and time spent outside the home, then the children will adjust just fine. The fact that one of the parents will actually stay in the home that has been the children's lifelong home does not mean that parent automatically gets full physical custody.

The ninth factor is the reasonable preference of the child, if and only if the court considers that the child is of an appropriate age to express a preference. The court will interview the children, and then they'll place a transcript of their discussion with the children about their preference in a sealed envelope, just in case it ever comes back on appeal. The divorcing parties are never told about the conversation between the judge and the children. This is a very stressful time for children. The court keeps the conversation regarding the children's preference from the parents because children don't want to make one parent feel bad, or they don't want another parent to be mad at them for their talk with the judge, or for telling what their preference is. The judge will give this factor a little more weight if the children are, let's say, 15 years old. The judge will have to discern the intentions of the child, too, because sometimes, the kids will play, or manipulate the situation depending on what they're trying to get out of it. The court does have experience with this, obviously, and they will be able to tell if games are being played. The interview with the children is done behind closed doors, in chambers, not in open court.

The tenth factor is the willingness and the ability of each of the parties to facilitate and encourage a close and continuing parent-child relationship between the child and the other parent. This factor is very important because parents are seldom equal on this factor. Inevitably, at the beginning of a divorce, one of the parents, whoever's trying to take advantage, will try their best to keep the child from seeing the other parent. This interference with the relationship is a very bad move by that parent. When a parent keeps a child from seeing the other parent until the temporary order is in place, it hurts their case, and isn't good for the child. They're not focusing on what's best for the child.

That parent is letting emotion drive their behavior to focus on hurting the other party. The court sees this behavior as being unwilling or unable to facilitate or encourage close parent-child relationships. I always encourage my clients to encourage and facilitate contact between the child and the other parent and to make sure it's documented. Sometimes the other parent will lie and say, "No, you never let me see them," when in fact, they said, "No, I'll take them some other day because I'm busy today." It is very important that parties put forth an effort to encourage that relationship and help that relationship to flourish, because that is what the law considers to be in the best interest of the children.

The eleventh factor is for the court to determine whether or not domestic violence has occurred, regardless of whether it was directed against or witnessed by the child. Domestic violence has a very broad definition in Michigan. "Domestic violence" just means an assault committed on a person who is a "family or household member." A "family or household member" includes a spouse or former spouse, a person with whom you are currently or have resided with, a person with whom you have had or are having a dating or sexual relationship, a person to whom you are related or have been by marriage, a person with whom you have a child in common, or any minor child of the persons described above.

Finally, the twelfth factor gives the judge the opportunity to determine whether there is anything else that is important to consider that is relevant to a particular child custody dispute.
The court will have to go through every single factor, regardless of whether some of the factors in a specific case are more important than others.

Divorce is a very difficult time no matter who you are or whether or not you wanted it. Everyone involved suffers. Try your best to be diplomatic because everyone who is important to you, including your children, will remember how you dealt with your divorce. Be the bigger person. Avoid the blame game. Be classy. Speed things up. Celebrate when it is all over.

Turn the page because you're about to write a new and better chapter in your life, because you can only go up from here. I promise you things will only get better if you play fair and smart.

(This content should be used for informational purposes only. It does not create an attorney-client relationship with any reader and should not be construed as legal advice. If you need legal advice, please contact an attorney in your community who can assess the specifics of your situation.)

Katherine Eisold Miller,
Katherine Eisold Miller PC
New Rochelle, NY

Katherine Eisold Miller is a prominent Collaborative lawyer and family mediator with a practice located in Westchester County and New York City, New York. After a decade of child welfare and matrimonial litigation, she abandoned the court system in search of a better way for families to resolve disputes. She has dedicated her career to educating the public about the importance of choosing a way to get divorced once the decision to divorce or separate is made. She advocates putting the needs of children first, respecting the parties and mitigating stress during the divorce process.

WHICH DIVORCE PROCESS IS BEST FOR ME?

When people face a divorce, whether they are the one choosing to end the marriage or not, they face a confusing array of emotions. Sadness, anger, disappointment, liberation, excitement, and more can all be mixed up together in a disorienting mess. Sometimes people feel shame and, almost always, they feel vulnerable and anxious.

Imagine this person facing divorce is you (and maybe you really are in this situation).

If you are like most people, you are likely, at least eventually, to go see a lawyer. Oftentimes the lawyer's name will come from a friend, colleague or family member. You will probably go see the lawyer and tell him or her your story. That will feel like a huge relief. Finally, you are in a place where someone listens to you without challenging or judging. The lawyer has heard so many other people's stories and knows how to respond in a way that makes you feel better. It is tempting to sign up with that person right then and there without exploring what services he or she offers. Before you do, there are some things you should know.

When you face divorce, the most important decision you make in the beginning is not what lawyer to hire. The most important decision is choosing what type of process to use in making the decisions required in the divorce. The process you will select (litigation, mediation, or collaboration), will impact your future relationship with your ex-spouse, your future co-parenting relationship, and in the end, your satisfaction with the final divorce judgment.

LITIGATION

Litigation is the most traditional way people work toward divorce. In this process, each person hires a lawyer and you proceed towards trial.

The irony is that 90–95 percent of cases never actually go to trial but are settled between the parties before a judge hands down a decision. That means that when most people start out on the path of litigation, they start working toward preparing for trial. They often engage in formal discovery procedures including depositions, interrogatories, and sometimes pre-trial motions and conferences. At the same time, their lawyers are trying to settle their divorce. They end up paying their lawyers to do two jobs. One is to prepare for trial. Lawyers must do that job in the litigation process, but the chances that you will actually go to trial are maybe four to ten percent.

The other task is trying to settle your case. So in effect, your lawyer is trying to do two things at the same time: prepare for trial and settle the case. The chances are good that you will settle your case, but most of the lawyer's activity will actually be focused on carrying out his or her professional responsibility to prepare for trial. It is likely to be very expensive but, statistically, will most likely end in settlement. The settlement may come because you have run out of money or patience or time, and it may not feel good but you are overwhelmingly likely to settle.

If you and your spouse want to focus on settlement from the very beginning rather than on trial preparation, you have two other options:

- Collaborative Divorce (also known as Collaborative Law or Collaborative Practice)

- Mediation

Collaborative dispute resolution and mediation have a number of marked advantages over traditional litigation, especially in emotionally difficult disputes. These methods minimize or eliminate court time, usually reduce fees, and avoid court-scheduling problems. Additionally, collaborative dispute resolution and mediation allow the parties to resolve their differences in private, as opposed to public court proceedings that on the record.

MEDIATION

Mediation is a facilitated conversation with the husband[1] and the wife and the mediator in a room. Over a series of sessions, the mediator helps the parties identify the issues that they need to resolve, gather the information they need in order to answer the questions that arise, and then work through a conversation where the questions are answered and a settlement is cobbled together. The mediator is often, but not always, a lawyer. In family mediations, the lawyers are not usually in the room during the mediation sessions but are readily available to provide the support of legal counsel.

The mediator or the attorneys then draft a settlement agreement, that will ultimately be reviewed by the attorneys and then executed by the parties. The process of mediation provides people with autonomy. The husband and wife are encouraged to speak for themselves in a room together with the mediator, which, for some people, is very empowering, and for others, very overwhelming.

COLLABORATIVE DIVORCE

Collaborative Divorce allows the couple, each advised by a Collaborative lawyer, to work toward a resolution in an informal and discreet setting. Without the burden of court-dictated formality and procedure, the parties are free to express their concerns and identify the issues most important to them. Collaborative Practice also gives people the chance to work with an interdisciplinary team of professionals who bring their expertise not only to the legal aspects of the conflict but also to the financial, emotional, and parenting issues. The attorneys are

---

[1] This text refers to the two spouses as husband and wife, although it is equally applicable to marriages with two husbands or two wives or other types of domestic partnerships.

disqualified from litigating so everyone in the room is focused entirely on settlement rather than on trial preparation.

If you think about the issues in a divorce as a tangled basket of different-colored yarns that a kitten got into. Each color represents one aspect of the divorce—emotional, financial, legal, parenting—all twisted together. The idea of the interdisciplinary collaborative approach is that people have the option to work with professionals (attorneys, accountants, psychologists, and social workers) who are collaboratively trained and professionally qualified to deal with legal, parenting, and financial issues. Each professional has a very specifically targeted problem-solving area of expertise, and each one can help address the issues that the people need to resolve. The group of experts identify the economic and social realities of the case, and look at what's important to the two people and to their children. The professional group works together, creating options that make sense for both parties and developing a resolution to the divorce that both parties can agree on.

HOW DO YOU KNOW WHAT PROCESS IS BEST FOR YOU?

Mediation is well-suited for people who have a fairly balanced relationship, where both people feel able to speak for themselves in the room. It's important that each person feel able to state his or her own view, and not to be constantly holding back because he or she is afraid of the other person's reaction. If there's a level of fear in the room, or if either party would be consistently uncomfortable without the support of an ally in the room other than the mediator, mediation may not work for them.

For people who feel comfortable stating their views and want to be able to deal directly with each other, mediation is a good choice because the couple can talk frankly, work out issues pertaining to the divorce, and feel real ownership over their process and over their result.

On the other end of the spectrum are people who cannot stand the idea of being in the same room with each other. I would say across the board, 99.5% of people are angry when they're getting a divorce. Anger is not a reason to choose litigation. However, where there is domestic violence, where there is real bullying or real fear of economic dishonesty or an impenetrable smokescreen, people might choose litigation. If you're already in court, and the other person refuses to do something other than litigate, then litigation is, of course, the obvious choice. Because mediation and Collaborative Divorce are voluntary processes, litigation is also the only choice when one party refuses to engage in any other process.

People choose Collaborative Divorce, when they want to work out the issues between themselves but feel the need for more support in doing so. They need somebody to help them make their voices heard in the room so that their needs are met, and they don't feel entirely comfortable doing that on their own. Because both people have their attorneys in the room, it can feel like having an ally. The attorney has your back and can make sure your concerns and objectives are addressed in the conversations. Collaborative Divorce also offers more structure and more obvious access to the non-attorney professionals.

WHAT IS THE DIFFERENCE IN COST WITH THE CHOICES?

The question of cost is one that everybody asks at the beginning of the divorce and one that's very difficult to answer, but I think that there are certain important things to consider. Choosing the appropriate process is really important from the very beginning. If you were to say, for instance, "I'm going to choose mediation because it's cheaper," you might be right but only if you reach a satisfactory conclusion. You could potentially spend thousands of dollars in mediation and not get anywhere, or not get as far as you'd hoped. It's important that you choose a process that is likely to work in your individual case, and it's important to think about the value you're getting for your dollars, not just the dollars that you're spending.

Litigation is often not a value-added process because so many divorces settle eventually, although not usually at the very beginning. They settle at a certain point in the process. In litigation, that point is often reached after an action has been filed, after several court appearances, and after some formal discovery has occurred. These things are helpful but are not necessarily the most efficient or least expensive way of getting the information or moving the case to a conclusion.

When people come into mediation, on the other hand, and their only reason for choosing mediation is to save money, I tell them I don't think it's going to work for them. That alone is not sufficient motivation for them to work together to try to reach a resolution. There has to be another emotional or psychological reason in order for them to be successful. For example, they may want to be good co-parents or be able to remain friends and minimize the disruption for their family. They really have to look at their motives for choosing a process and determine if that process is the best way for them to achieve their goals.

CHILD CUSTODY ISSUES

Regardless of their situation, when people come into my office to talk about divorce, the first thing that we talk about is process choice. The second thing is what issues are they going to have to resolve? What is the scope of this divorce conversation? It usually comes down to three areas; those are parenting, division of assets and liabilities, and cash flow.

Parenting involves two concepts: decision-making and time sharing. Decision-making is determining how the parents are going to make the important decisions concerning health, education, and welfare of their kids. They can choose to make all decisions together, one parent can be the decision maker, or they can divide decision-making into spheres of influence. For example, one parent makes secular education decisions and the other makes religious education decisions.

Time sharing has two aspects: regular time and special time. Regular time is weekdays and weekends. How are you going to share parenting time Monday through Friday? What are you going to do about the weekends? Special time is holidays and vacations. How are you going to handle the holidays that each family celebrates? How are you going to handle the children's school vacations? How are you going to handle summer vacations and birthdays?

One advantage of being in a non-litigation process is that you can start thinking about parenting in people terms rather than in legal terms. If you think about it, the terms decision making and time sharing have really different emotional connotations than does the term "child custody." Nobody wants to "lose custody" of their kids. People feel more comfortable dealing with "decision making" and "time sharing," than they do with "custody." Consequently, many people are able to make health, education, and welfare decisions together even if they're really at odds with each other. When parents are able to make decisions together, it is good for their kids. We call that joint legal custody.

The other issue is time sharing. Where are the kids when? What makes the most sense for them? How are the parents going to share their time? How have they spent holidays and vacations? We work together to make decisions about the children's regular time and special time working toward a parenting plan that is supportive and nurturing for the children.

One of the most painful parts of divorce is not being with your children. For people who celebrate Christmas, not having your kids on Christmas day is heart breaking. Not having them every Thanksgiving can be horrifying. Facing the reality that life will never be the same for your kids or yourselves is a challenge. How will you manage that challenge? It will be much better for your children if you can find a way to work through the pain and let go of the resentment you might feel.

Parents have to be flexible and adjust their plan for the evolving needs of their children. A parenting plan that works for a four-year-old and a six-year-old isn't going to work anymore when they are 14 and 16, because the children will have changed. Hopefully, the final divorce document will have enough flexibility to allow the parents to be able to work together and adapt to the family's needs as the children mature. It's much easier to do that if, during the divorce process itself, the parents are able to learn to work together to find a resolution that makes sense for the children.

There are no two people in the world who are going to love your children the way you and their other parent—your ex-spouse—do. No one else on the face of the planet is going to feel the same way toward them, so it's nice to have a process that allows you to enjoy your children together, even if you're divorced, and to co-parent them in a way that feels supportive of each other going forward.

DIVISION OF ASSETS AND LIABILITIES ISSUES

Division of assets and liabilities means basically figuring out what you have, what you owe, the nature of the property (meaning is it marital or separate), and then how you're going to divide it up. In the United States, you either live in an equitable distribution state or in a community property state, but the question is the same. What's in a marital estate? What's it worth? What's its nature, and then how are we going to divide it up?

Every divorce goes through an information-gathering stage. We work to find a shared understanding of the family's economic reality. What is there and what is it worth? And what is the nature of the asset? Is it an investment account? Is it a more complex type of compensation vehicle, like a restrictive stock unit or stock option, that may or may not be vested, that may have certain future requirements before the titled spouse is vested? Is it transferrable? Are the retirement assets qualified plans or non-qualified plans?

Sometimes people own businesses. The business could be owned by just one party and sometimes a couple is in business together. With a co-owned business, the parties may want to divide the business or they may want to stay in it together. There are situations where people have a business that they own and run together, and their marriage is ending, but they don't want to end their business partnership. We have to work out a way that allows them to formalize the business relationship at the same time that we're working through their divorce, and we're detangling their assets.

Sometimes, cases are more complicated, especially with people in higher net-worth situations, or people who have come from family wealth, where there may be trusts and various other complex estate planning tools that go back generations. Other times, it's really very simple.

When choosing your divorce process, an important point to consider is that litigation is a public proceeding. At trial, virtually anyone can walk into the back of the courtroom and sit down and hear testimony about your case. It varies from state to state, i.e., the file is more or less protected by state rules, but in some states, anybody can go in, request to see the file and see all the assets and liabilities. In other states, the files are sealed. The degree of privacy depends on your state's rules.

On the other hand, Collaborative Divorce and mediation are 100 percent private. In addition, in Collaborative Divorce and in mediation, instead of expensive and time-consuming court-directed formal discovery procedures that we talked about earlier (notices of discovery and inspection, motion practice, depositions, and interrogatories) everyone makes a voluntary commitment that each person will share all relevant information and that the information will be private within the process and only used to reach the settlement.

Oftentimes, people choose litigation because they feel that it offers more protection than Collaborative Divorce or mediation. I think that there may actually be more opportunity, in a non-litigation setting, to actually access true information.

I think that probably 85 percent of people can work successfully in the Collaborative Divorce process, and at least 40 percent of people could work in a mediation process, probably more than that. That leaves a pretty small portion of people facing a divorce who really need to litigate for reasons having to do with their own personal situation.

IN THE END, MOST PEOPLE DO WANT TO BE FAIR IN A DIVORCE

Often, in a divorce, there's animosity, but not malevolence. I actually am hard-pressed to think of a single divorce case in my entire career where a client has consistently said to me, "I don't want to be fair," meaning, "I really want an unfair result. I really want my husband to live in a cardboard box on the street so I can stay in the marital home." Most people want to be fair, even though they're angry, and they may want the person to hurt, but they also want them to be okay. I think it's important for most people to feel that they treated the other person fairly and were treated fairly in return, because they want to see themselves as the good people that they are.

PSYCHOLOGICAL ASPECTS OF DIVORCE

Psychologically, divorce is a very trying time in anybody's life. There are a lot of emotions that cause suffering: anger, jealousy, betrayal, and fear. There's also, underlying it, guilt, shame, and vulnerability; and sometimes, a sense of opportunity or freedom or excitement about getting to do something different.

I think that people really need to find a way to give themselves the support and time that they need to sort through a divorce. Granted, this is a trying time, but if they can start to get some sense of what the future holds and where they want to go—not reactively, but focused on their wishes, hopes and dreams—with help, they can start to focus on those goals in the divorce process. If they are willing to look to the future, we can create a divorce settlement that focuses them toward their wishes, hopes, and dreams for the future, in a way that's really constructive rather than destructive.

Every person is different, and people approach conflict in very individualized ways. Every marriage has a conflict pattern and by the time you decide to divorce it's probably not working very well. The professionals you are working with can help you recognize the nature of the conflict dynamic in the family. Oftentimes, when I ask people, "When you were married, how did you resolve conflict?" a stunning number them say, "We didn't have conflict." What that means to me is that they didn't resolve conflict. It means that people are entering into a negotiation that's going to impact their lives, their children's lives, and their future in a way unlike any other; and they don't know how to resolve conflict together.

They will have to learn to resolve conflict as part of the divorce and maybe for the future. If children are involved, we need to help the parents learn how to have conflict conversations in a way that works. This is where the interdisciplinary collaborative approach can really be useful. The collaborative mental health professionals are highly skilled individuals, and trained to help people work through these conflict conversations.

CASH FLOW

One of the first things that we do in the divorce process is figure out the cost of the lifestyle that the people had while they were married. What did they spend money on, and where did that money come from? Essentially, we are measuring the cost of their standard of living as it currently exists or as it existed when they lived together. Then we do an analysis. When they live separately, will there be enough money coming into the family unit to cover their same lifestyle in separate households? If there is enough, then we just need to figure out the cash flow, but if there isn't (and there usually isn't), then we have to make some decisions about how we're going to address that lack of funds.

One way that there may be cash flow from one parent to the other is through child support. In a litigation setting, it's paid from the "non-custodial parent" to the "custodial parent," meaning it's paid from the parent who has less time with the children to the parent who has more time with the children. Sometimes that means that the higher earning parent pays child support to the lower earning parent. The children will usually spend more time with one parent who has spent more time at home and less time in the workplace.

Child support is usually paid to cover the basic living expenses of the children. Every state has a statute that specifies a percentage of the combined parental incomes to be used for child support and dictates some factors that the court must apply. Judges can deviate from the formula based on certain factors. It's important to understand that child support is non-deductible for the payer and non-taxable to the payee, and it's for basic living expenses such as food, shelter, and clothing for the kids. Obviously, there are some expenses that are shared with the parent, like the roof over the children's head. Child support is payable from inception to emancipation of the child or children at age 18 or 21, depending on the state, or at an agreed-upon time. In New York, the emancipation age is 21, but people often will agree that emancipation occurs at 22 or upon graduation from college. This keeps the child support going throughout the children's college education.

Alimony, sometimes called maintenance or spousal support, is paid from a higher earning spouse to a lower earning spouse for that lower earning spouse's support. Spousal support, or alimony, is deductible to the payer and includable in the recipient's income for tax purposes. In many states, depending on the case, the judge, the mood, the day, the year, the weather, you could get widely varying alimony determinations. Judges may not like to hear that, but it's true.

I like to use the term "cash flow" rather than alimony or child support because people often have an emotional reaction to the legal terms. When you go to the supermarket to buy food, you either have money in your wallet or you don't. When you open up your wallet to pay, there are no dividers between the money you received from working or from alimony or child support. It's about cash—you can continue living the life the way you've been living it or you can't. That's what we really need to look at, and it's much more productive than trying to compartmentalize funds for either child support or alimony. We need to make sure the kids of the marriage and both parents are going to be okay going forward given the facts of their lives.

At this moment in history, 95 percent of alimony payers are men. It can be challenging when the wife makes considerably more money than the husband and she is the major breadwinner of the family. This is especially true if she thinks her husband is not doing his share domestically. I'm talking about a situation where she thinks she has arranged all the child care, she has managed their medical care, and she has arranged for play dates. She's been the person they called when they needed a ride even though she was at work. In addition to all that, she also paid the bills. She is responsible for 90–100 percent of their assets. She may be resentful that she would have to divide those assets with him and possibly pay support to him to give him a chance to get on his feet. Of course, her husband will have a different perspective on his role in the family and it may well be that this conflict has contributed to the end of the marriage.

In my experience, when women have to pay alimony, the women feel incredibly resentful, and the men don't like to receive it because it seems emasculating. It's not what we expect culturally. But clearly, that's going to have to change as women become a stronger force in the workplace and earn more money, and we have fewer traditional type families.

PRENUPTIAL AGREEMENTS

Many people consider prenuptial agreements as anti-marriage, anti-romantic, and disruptive to the marital dynamic in advance of the wedding. I have had many colleagues, who have sat at meetings representing clients in prenuptial discussions, basically say to the clients, "Do you really need this? Do you really want this? Is this really a good thing?" meaning that, in their opinion, it's not. I think that's really crazy because here's the thing:

> *Your marriage is going to come to an end, whether it's by death or by divorce.*

So since you know your marriage is going to end, why not think about that a little bit in advance? Why not talk in advance of the wedding about your expectations concerning your financial roles and parenting roles in the marriage? Why not have a conversation about that in advance, before you're in the marriage? I think it makes a lot of sense to do that in a mediation or collaboration setting, where you have support, and communication between the couple is emphasized. The idea of a prenuptial agreement as a conversation about money and about pre-planning the end of the marriage, whether by divorce or by death, really makes sense.

I really try to encourage people to understand that asking for a pre-nuptial agreement does not mean that they're selfish or controlling or difficult. Instead, they're really being careful and thoughtful and proactive about planning for their marriage. Unfortunately, this is not the way it usually happens. The more common scenario goes something like this:

> *You and I are getting married. I have some assets. You may or may not, but you haven't really thought about it. You don't think*

it's romantic. In order for us to get married, my parents insist that we have this agreement. We argue about it. You finally agree. I go to my lawyer. My lawyer writes something up that has to do with these conversations with me and maybe with my family. You go on thinking maybe I forgot it, and you're thinking, "I would like pink for the napkins, it will go with the roses that the men will be wearing in their buttonholes going down the aisle. And maybe we should have the chicken chardonnay, or maybe it should be the salmon." You're thinking about the wedding planning, and I'm thinking about the wedding planning, but I'm also thinking about this prenuptial.

Then a while before we get married, I say, "Alright, my lawyer has this draft. Here it is. He said you really need a lawyer." And now, what's your fiancée's reaction to that? Her reaction is, "Wait a second. I was thinking about the wedding. I agreed to do this, but I have to have a lawyer? I have to pay money for this now?" So then maybe months pass before she finally gets around to hiring a lawyer because she doesn't think it's romantic, and it just feels like a real disruption to your relationship. Finally, she hires a lawyer. The lawyer waits for the prenuptial agreement, which you haven't read because you can't stand to, and then her lawyer says, "Oh my God. I can't believe they're asking for this."

That is the tone of the typical prenuptial conversation. On the other hand, the conversation could go like this:

"You know what, Honey? We're getting married in six months, and I think it would really make sense for us to talk about our expectations for our financial contributions to our family in the future. What's going to happen in the event that we get a divorce or one of us dies during the marriage, how would we deal with that? I'd like to have a conversation with

these people who can advise us, in a mediator's office or with a collaborative attorney."

Or,

"I'm feeling a lot of pressure from my family, and I'd like to engage you in a conversation about how we're going to deal with some issues, before we get married."

I think that sets a really different tone, and I would really encourage people to consider that. A lot of people say that the two biggest reasons for divorce are money problems or money disagreements and sex. I think communication problems really underlie most divorces. Either way, since money is such a big issue between couples and, in our society, why wouldn't we talk about money before we got married?

Acceptance of a prenuptial agreement often depends on the way the idea is presented. My mother-in-law had a prenuptial agreement with her second husband, and it brought out an interesting perspective. As in all marriages, some challenging situations developed. She later said, "The prenuptial agreement kept me in the marriage because I didn't have fantasies about how I was going to punish him and walk away with all the money. I knew exactly what I was going to get, and that's what kept me at it and successfully so."

(This content should be used for informational purposes only. It does not create an attorney-client relationship with any reader and should not be construed as legal advice. If you need legal advice, please contact an attorney in your community who can assess the specifics of your situation.)

Daniel C. Hunter IV
The Hunter Law Group
Mission Viejo, CA

Daniel Hunter recognizes the fragility of the situation and we can help by fighting for your rights, your goals, and above all, your child's best interests. It is important to recognize that although he is extremely savvy when it comes to handling legal procedures, he does not let that get in the way of providing personalized attention. As an attorney who truly cares about you and your family, he will investigate your situation as something that is unique, not merely treating it as just another case.

WHEN IT'S OVER, IT'S OVER... OR IS IT?

The first step in the divorce process is realizing that the marriage is over. One or both parties may come to the realization that the problems in their marriage are irremediable. Once one or both of the parties makes this determination, the next step requires one of the parties to take action and begin the process of dissolving the marriage. This action may be formal or informal. For example, one party may move out of the marital residence, begin to separate finances, or actually file a Petition for dissolution of marriage. The point being that one or both of the parties must come to the realization that the marriage is over and that reconciliation is not possible or not desired. This leads to one party beginning the process of dissolving the marriage.

I consider dissolving a marriage to be more of a process than an event and encourage my clients to do the same. All divorces, regardless of whether children are involved, are simply a restructuring or reorganization of the family and finances. However, a divorce involving children is always more difficult because while you may be severing your marital bond, you will be connected to your spouse through your children for the rest of your or your spouse's natural life. A couple without children has a much easier time severing all ties and leading separate lives. However, even without children, some support obligation may require some financial connection for a period of time. Therefore, it is important to view a divorce as a process rather than an event.

Regardless of whether children are involved, the parties have a duty to disclose all financial information about their assets, debts, and investment opportunities to the other party as they work through the process of dissolving their marriage and separating their finances. The penalties for less-than-full disclosure are too great. To make the divorce process more efficient, a client should be honest and disclose all information that his or her attorney requests. This will help you and the attorney strategize both litigation positions and potential settlement strategies.

TEMPORARY OR INTERIM ORDERS

Upon filing a petition for dissolution of marriage, the court will generally issue a series of temporary orders on the issues of custody, visitation, and financial support. This allows the parties to participate in discovery, or the exchange of information, and identification of issues for trial or settlement. Generally speaking, the court wants ensure that both parties have the opportunity to retain legal counsel to advise them of their rights as they work through the divorce process and related issues toward a final and permanent resolution. If the parties are able to settle all issues without the need for court intervention, they may present a settlement agreement to the court and it will adopt the agreement and enter it as a final judgment. However, in order for the judgment to be valid and not subject to being overturned, it must be free from fraud and duress, as well as dispose of all marital issues, If the parties disagree on some or all of the issues, the case will proceed through the discovery phase and on to trial. At trial, the judge (as opposed to a jury) will hear evidence and argument from both parties and then make a final determination on all of the issues before the court. Even after a final judgment has been entered the court retains jurisdiction to adjudicate certain matters such as omitted assets and debts as well as to enforce the judgment. In cases that involve minor children, the court also retains jurisdiction to modify custody and visitation because life brings constant change and it is always interested in what is best for the children. Often times, a divorce isn't over even after it's over.

PRESERVING PARENT–CHILD RELATIONSHIPS

The most difficult part of a divorce often involves the legal and physical custody or parental time of the minor children. The court presumes that it is in the children's best interest for parents to share in the child rearing responsibilities. It also presumes that frequent and continuing contact with both parents is in the children's best interest. In determining custody and visitation decisions, the courts seek to make orders that are in the best interest of the child. Therefore, judges consider all relevant evidence regarding the health, safety, and welfare of the child. There is no presumption that one parent should have more time with the child than the other parent. Therefore, the judge takes into consideration a variety of factors when determining custody and visitation such as the age of the child, which parent has been the primary caregiver, the work schedules of each parent, the child's school, compliance with court orders, and which parent is most likely to support a relationship between the child and the other parent.

A judge will also consider factors that may be detrimental to the child's best interest when determining custody and visitation. For example, if one parent is actively trying to alienate the child from the other parent the court may find this conduct detrimental to the child and award the non-offending party custody. Some examples of alienating behavior include: speaking derogatorily about the other parent in the presence of the child or allowing others to do so, interfering with the other party's parental time, undermining the authority of the other parent, or doing anything else that disrupts or damages the relationship between the child and the other parent. Parents should be fostering a healthy relationship between their child and the other parent even though the parties are no longer in a happy marriage. Be forewarned that attempts to alienate a child from the other parent, whether intentional or not, by pointing out the other parent's behavior or blaming the other parent for the divorce can often backfire when the parties meet in the courtroom.

Domestic violence is a tragic and unfortunate element of some divorces. When the allegation of domestic violence is present, the judge will consider this factor when determining custody and visitation orders that are in the child's best interest. Courts consider the commission of domestic violence by one parent against the other to be detrimental to the child and when committed in the presence of the child it is considered especially egregious. Depending on the circumstances, such cases can result in one parent being awarded sole legal and physical custody of the child on a permanent basis. Often times, such facts warrant one parent having sole legal and physical custody, at least on a temporary basis, until the court is able to hear further evidence from both parties, an expert, and/or an investigator. It could also result in the judge granting only supervised visitation with the alleged offending parent pending a formal hearing or trial on the issues. The court's ultimate goal is to do what is in the child's best interest both on a temporary basis as the parties go through the fact-finding process and on a permanent basis once all of the issues have been settled or litigated. It will generally err on the side of caution when making orders by protecting the child from the credible risk of domestic violence or abduction.

INSIGHTS INTO CHILD SUPPORT

The issue of child support can also be a contentious issue. The law draws a very bright line between child support issues on the one hand versus custody and visitation issues on the other hand. They are two separate and distinct issues that are handled completely separately. In other words, the parent ordered to pay child support cannot be denied visitation if he or she should fall behind on their support obligations. A parent is never justified in withholding visitation because the other parent is not meeting his or her support obligation. Make no mistake, the court has many tools at its disposal, including putting a party in jail, for failure to pay support. However, it cannot make custody and visitation decisions based on a party's failure to meet the support obligations. Simply stated, a parent that resorts to self-help remedies such as withholding visitation for failure to pay support jeopardizes his or her own custodial rights. Parent–child relationships are priceless and courts are ever cognizant of this principle.

The court considers the gross income of each parent in relation to the amount of time the child spends in each household. It wants to ensure that the child's needs are met in each household. Therefore, if a child spends the majority of their time with one parent the other parent will pay an amount of child support that equalizes the financial burden of rearing the child, taking time spent actually caring for the child into account. As stated, the purpose of child support is to ensure that the child's needs are being adequately met in both homes. Both parties have an obligation to support the child and the court will use its powers to ensure that both parents have relatively equal access to resources needed to care for the child.

DIVIDING THE MARITAL ESTATE

Spouses have a fiduciary duty to each other. This requires both parties to fully disclose all assets and obligations to one another. This duty exists during the marriage (whether or not it is observed is another matter) and continues until the estate is fully adjudicated. Unfortunately, some parties may try to hide or intentionally undervalue assets in an attempt to obtain an economic advantage over the other. This can more easily occur in marriages where one spouse managed or controlled the finances throughout the marriage. It can be tempting for the managing spouse to hide or incorrectly value assets and debts. However, the court takes the parties' fiduciary duty to disclose all marital assets and debts completely and accurately very seriously; and the penalties for hiding assets, misstating debts, or misrepresenting their real value can be harsh. In fact, a judge can award the non-offending spouse one hundred percent (100%) of the undisclosed or undervalued asset plus attorney's fees and costs incurred to uncover the deception and bring it to the court's attention. A court may also award punitive damages in some cases where the offending party's conduct is intentional and oppressive. In other words, if a spouse willfully and intentionally tries to hide assets to deceive the court and the other spouse, the judge could penalize the offending party by awarding the other party an amount greater than one hundred percent of the value of the asset (i.e., three times or more the value of the asset).

A good attorney will thoroughly evaluate the disclosure of assets and debts and will engage other professionals when necessary to assist in this evaluation process. Strategy and negotiation remain paramount even in the face of full and fair disclosure. A good attorney will also obtain supporting documentation to accurately evaluate the thoroughness and accuracy of the other party's disclosures.

POST-JUDGMENT MODIFICATION

Even when a final decree or judgment has been entered, there still may be situations in which a modification may be appropriate. The reasons for seeking to modify a final decree or judgment vary greatly. Different standards apply when seeking to modify a judgment, depending on the type of modification sought. For example, if support is to be modified, the court will need to see a change in circumstances that warrant such a modification like losing one's job. While the courts desire judgments to be fixed in order to provide finality, they do recognize that life is fluid and changes do occur that will warrant the modification of a final order. The most common modifications involve custody, visitation, and support due to changes in employment and other life events.

BANKRUPTCY DURING DIVORCE PROCEEDINGS

In today's economy, bankruptcy has become more common. Some spouses even file for bankruptcy during the pendency of a divorce. While the filing of a bankruptcy petition will not necessarily stop the divorce proceedings, it can create issues that may slow down or complicate the divorce process. For example, one spouse's filing for bankruptcy relief could raise the issue of fraudulent transfer in the eyes of creditors. Typically, this scenario arises when the family court divides the community assets and liabilities in such a manner that one spouse assumes more than one-half of the community debt and the other receives a greater portion of the marital assets. In the event that the party being assigned the debt seeks to discharge the same in bankruptcy court, the transfer of assets and assignment of debts may be set aside. Creditors are given this power under the Uniform Fraudulent Transfers Act. Similarly, if one spouse knowingly accepts an unequal division of debt in order to obtain some other offset or benefit for doing so, only to promptly turn around and discharge that debt in bankruptcy court, that spouse is acting in bad faith and breaching his or her fiduciary duty to the other spouse. This is another example of why full disclosure is important during the divorce process. Moreover, communication between the divorce attorney and the bankruptcy attorney is essential when a client or the opposing party files for bankruptcy during a divorce.

If both spouses are liable for a debt under the terms of a loan they both signed, the creditor may pursue either party to be made whole, regardless of which spouse is assigned the debt in the divorce proceeding. The creditor will typically seek to enforce the contract against the higher-earning spouse. Therefore, it is important to have the party assigned the debt indemnify and hold the other party harmless. It is also important to get legal advice in managing debt early in the proceedings.

If a spouse is contemplating filing for bankruptcy during divorce, they should seek the advice of an experienced bankruptcy attorney. A good divorce attorney should have some basic knowledge of bankruptcy law. However, bankruptcy is a specialized area of the law. A good family law attorney will know his or her boundaries and advise their client when he should seek the advice of a competent bankruptcy attorney. Again, communication between the family law attorney and the bankruptcy attorney is crucial to ensure proper treatment of division of assets and debts.

INSIGHTS INTO RELOCATION ISSUES

Another issue that arises during or even after a divorce proceeding is the possibility of one spouse's desire to relocate. As soon as you believe relocation may be an issue, you need to notify your attorney. Courts typically frown on making a request to move away shortly after the divorce decree becomes final. Therefore, it is usually best to address this issue up front, as soon as it arises. Although the courts understand there are times when relocation is sudden due to a change in circumstances, if you have an idea you want to relocate or may need to do so, it is imperative that you address the issue as soon as it arises. Courts also frown on self-help remedies, such as fleeing the state with the child immediately prior to the divorce being filed or moving away with the child after the decree is final without first obtaining court permission or a written agreement authorizing the move. The Uniform Child Custody Jurisdiction Enforcement Act prohibits this conduct. Regardless, jurisdiction battles are not uncommon and need to be resolved before any other issue. Many states will not exercise jurisdiction, so this issue must be addressed first.

When a parent fails to address the issue of relocation before moving away with the child, the court will almost inevitably issue an order to return the child to the "home state," even though the parent moving may truly believe that he or she was acting in the best interest of the child. Such conduct is hard on the child as well as the parents. It causes needless turmoil in the life of the child and all others involved. The correct course of action is to address the issue in such a way that the court can look at all relevant factors in deciding what is in the best interest of the child. Because we live in a transitory world, meaning that we move frequently due to a sophisticated inter-state commerce system, making it relatively inexpensive to travel, it is very common for parents and children to relocate. However, the initial custody order may make moving easier for one parent over the other depending on the findings and orders. For example, if a parent has sole physical custody of the minor child, it may make moving easier in the future. Likewise, if the non-custodial parent has minimal contact with the child and is less involved in the child's life than the custodial parent, it may also make it easier for the custodial parent to move. It is important to take all of this into consideration during the divorce process. This is why it is important to have a skilled attorney assist you in the process. Without one, you may create a serious problem that will only become apparent at an urgent moment in a parent's life and career.

There are different burdens of proof that an attorney must consider when requesting an order allowing the child to relocate with one parent. In some cases, the court will look to see if the move would be detrimental to the child. In others it will look to see if a move is in the child's best interest. There is a distinction between determining the best interest of a child versus considering the adverse effects on a parent–child relationship or even an actual showing of detriment to the child. If the judgment results joint legal and joint physical custody with equal parenting time and one parent seeks to move away with the child, the court will use a *"trial de novo"* or a "blank slate" to evaluate a parent's request to move away with the child. The judge will not presume that one spouse has the right to relocate with the child. Whereas, in the instance of a parent that has the sole legal and sole physical custody of a child while the other parent spends minimal time with the child, the non-moving parent would be shouldered with the much higher burden of proving the proposed move would be detrimental to the child. Attorneys should consult with their clients to ensure that, during the divorce process, they are not setting themselves up for an almost insurmountable burden in the future if the other party wants to relocate with the child.

PRENUPTIAL AGREEMENTS

When I am asked about prenuptial agreements, I tell my clients that they can be very useful tools and appropriate in many cases. Prenuptial agreements are very common in second marriages or in marriages later in life where one or both parties have accumulated assets and financial stability that they want to protect. Prenuptial agreements can even provide for the creation of community property under certain conditions, so not only are they useful to protect assets that are being brought into a marriage in the event of a divorce, but they can also establish clear circumstances in which community property can be established. One example of when it may be appropriate to create a community property interest in an asset may be for the purchase of a vacation property. In this instance, it should be clear that when the parties take title to the property, it should be clearly stated that it is community property. Premarital agreements must be clear and they require complete and fair disclosure on the part of both parties. Both parties must have separate counsel review the agreement and advise them of their rights and responsibilities under the agreement. Agreements that are entered into without fair and complete disclosure can be set aside as unenforceable, especially when one spouse is waiving his or her right to spousal support. The courts consider waiving spousal support to be a very serious matter and the party waiving his or her rights in this regard should understand fully what he or she is giving up. If there is a finding that the spouse did not knowingly and intelligently waive support, the court can set aside the waiver.

Courts regularly enforce prenuptial agreements but the agreements must meet the basic requirements under the law. You need to retain the counsel who has experience drafting prenuptial agreements. You must also give the other person time to retain counsel and review the agreement with his or her own attorney well in advance of the wedding day. In other words, you cannot "spring" a prenuptial agreement on your spouse-to-be on the day of your wedding. There must be full disclosure and adequate time to seek independent counsel. In most states, there are statutory time requirements that constitute this reasonable time period. If you do not adhere to these requirements, the prenuptial agreement could be ruled unenforceable.

GRANDPARENT RIGHTS

The dynamics of families are changing rapidly in today's world and the courts now recognize grandparent rights as something protectable under the law. Today, some grandparents are very involved in raising grandchildren, especially when the child's life experiences a turn of events that gives rise to the need of the support and assistance of grandparents. These grandchildren have a close bond with their grandparents and that bond is important or even vital to the well-being of the child. In other words, it is in the best interest of the child to protect this bond, which is the basis for grandparent rights.

Regardless of the depth of the bond, grandparent rights are always going to be secondary to parental rights. Grandparent rights are typically not an issue because most parents want to foster a close, loving relationship between their child and his or her grandparents. When grandparent rights come to the forefront, most frequently, a parent has had a falling out with his or her parents and this rift extends to the grandchild. The parent may then use denial of visitation with the grandchildren as a weapon against the grandparent. Grandparents may then choose to assert their rights in a court of law. The grandparents can be joined to an existing case or commence an entirely new matter in order to assert their rights to a continued relationship with a grandchild with whom they have developed a close, loving relationship.

Oftentimes, alcohol, drugs, or mental health issues give rise to grandparent right cases. It is not hard to imagine circumstances in which a grandparent may naturally seek to intervene to protect a grandchild from behaviors stemming from alcohol and drug abuse or untreated mental health issues. Regardless, grandparent rights are distinguishable from parental rights and if the parent gets treatment for the addiction or mental health issue, the court will give him or her first priority in the child's life.

SAME-SEX MARRIAGE

Many states now recognize same-sex marriages and the U.S. Supreme Court made history by recognizing marriage as a fundamental right and stated that same-sex couples have a right to marry. Whether you agree with same-sex marriage or not, the dynamics of a family have changed in the United States. Therefore, in California, there is no difference between the divorce of same-sex couples and heterosexual couples. Theoretically, a same-sex couple's divorce would not look any different—the court would still deal with the issues of custody, support and the division of assets. Where I see an issue arising is a situation in which the same-sex couple is married in a state that recognizes same-sex marriages, then moves to a state that does not recognize same-sex marriages and files for divorce. Initial cases indicate states that do not have laws recognizing same-sex marriages maintain that they do not have jurisdiction (authority) to dissolve the marriage nor adjudicate the accompanying issues.

A similar problem arising in today's legal world is one in which a same-sex couple divorces in a state that recognizes same-sex marriages and thereafter one of the parties moves to a state that does not recognize same-sex marriages. Will that state register and enforce the divorce decree in the event that the party needing to register it for some reason such as enforcing visitation or child support? The state may have an interest in recognizing and enforcing the judgment from California under The Uniform Child Custody Jurisdiction Enforcement Act even though the state does not recognize the marriage because it has a vested interest in protecting the interests of the child. We will continue to see these types of issues because the scenarios are endless and jurisdiction will continue to be a problem so long as we have states that do not recognize the same-sex laws of other states.

These harsh but real results leave the same-sex couple and their family in a serious predicament. Same-sex marriage is still a relatively new frontier in the legal field, but I anticipate the issues will be addressed fairly and in relatively short-order because, as a society, we need to have consistent mechanisms for dealing with situations like these as same-sex marriages become recognized across the country.

LEGAL SEPARATION OR DIVORCE

I am often asked about the difference between a divorce and a separation. Some people may feel a legal separation is not as final as a divorce and this helps them emotionally deal with their failed marriage. That said, legal separation and divorce are two different legal animals.

A legal separation is one step short of a divorce in that the assets and liabilities are divided; custody and visitation orders are made and support is ordered. However, neither party is returned to single status. One reason a petition for legal separation rather than divorce might filed is in the event that one of the spouses has a pre-existing illness, such as cancer, and perhaps is receiving treatments under the other spouse's health insurance. Severing the marriage would terminate the insurance and, in all likelihood, the medical treatments. However, no state can force an individual to remain married. Therefore, if one spouse decides he or she has met his or her soul-mate, he or she can proceed with a dissolution of marriage action and sever the marital status, thereby returning the parties to single status.

Legal separation should also be distinguished from what is referred to as the "date of separation" in a marriage. The date of separation occurs when one of the spouses decides that an irreconcilable breakdown of the marriage has occurred and there is no chance of saving the marriage. From this point (the date of separation) forward, the parties earnings and debts become their separate property. It is important to have a basic understanding of these three terms: legal separation, divorce, and date of separation.

(This content should be used for informational purposes only. It does not create an attorney-client relationship with any reader and should not be construed as legal advice. If you need legal advice, please contact an attorney in your community who can assess the specifics of your situation.)

Kaine Fisher
Scottsdale, AZ

Kaine has focused his practice on representing clients in high-conflict, high-asset family law matters. He serves as a Vanguard Member for Sojourner Center, a domestic violence shelter and he is also on the Board of Directors for the Children's Advocacy League. He was named the "Best Attorney to have on your side to end things" by Scottsdale Living.

WISHES OF CHILDREN IN A DIVORCE

A frequent question I am asked as a divorce attorney is, "When are my child's wishes taken into consideration when it comes to deciding child custody in my divorce?"

Historically, a judge might talk to a child in his chambers. He might try his best to create an environment of comfort for the child. Although he would take off his robe, nothing seemed to take away from the anxiety the child experienced while sitting in a judge's chambers in a courthouse being grilled about his or her parents. These days, courts are hesitant to interview a child in chambers. Thankfully, Judges at some point began to realize the inherently intimidating nature of this practice and recognize there are professionals out there who are much more qualified than them to gather information about a child's thoughts, wishes, and desires. At least in Maricopa County, courts now defer this sensitive fact-gathering responsibility to mental health professionals in a very controlled and comfortable setting. We can now all breathe a sigh of relief that times have changed, and that judges now are more in tune with their limitations, and thus are leaving these delicate interactions with children up to the experts – mental health professionals who are educated, trained and experienced in the art of talking to children about sensitive issues.

Most people understand that divorce is tough on kids. As attorneys, we try our best to keep the kids out of the litigation so as to minimize the impact that a split is going to have on them. But realistically, sometimes involving the children to some degree is inevitable.

Unlike a small number of states, and contrary to the general public's perception in this state, Arizona does not have a bright line age at which the Court is required to consider the child's wishes solely determinative. Rather, in Arizona, the Court considers a total of 11 specific factors when rendering a decision about legal decision-making and parenting time. Comprehensively this is known as a "best interest of the child" determination, and one of the factors the Court considers is the child's wishes as to legal decision-making and parenting time.

For many years, the law simply required a court to consider "a child's wishes." Notably, however, the law in Arizona (as of January 1, 2013) requires a court to now first consider whether a child is of "suitable age and maturity" before taking into consideration his/her wishes. Whether a child is of "suitable age and maturity" is determined on a case-by-case basis. This is a significant change and how this additional requirement plays out is yet to be completely understood. Certainly, the Court will review the child's ability to effectively convey their thoughts and wishes to the interviewer, and will also consider whether the child has any physical or cognitive disabilities that may impact his/her maturity level. For instance, the child might have a disability that makes that particular child less mature than other children that same age. It may for obvious reasons not be appropriate to consider an interview with the child under these circumstances. However, once this threshold has been crossed, judges are free to consider the child's wishes when making a decision as they wish.

Judges are making decisions that could alter the course of a child's life. Their decisions can have long-lasting consequences. Consequently, I think most judges would agree that having more information is better than having less. Furthermore, Arizona does not have juries in family law matters. The judges decide. And judges have great legal minds. Certainly, they are able to effectively differentiate between what information is accurate and germane to the case, and what information may not be relevant or credible. They can very quickly discern whether they can take what the child says as gospel or not.

Looking at what a child wants is only one piece of the puzzle – thankfully so in my opinion. Some 15-year-olds don't know what's in their own best interest. They want to go and hang out with their friends whenever they want, stay out late, and play video games rather than have structure. Some kids like to go to Mom's house because Mom doesn't have as many rules, and they don't have to do as many chores. Maybe Dad is more of a disciplinarian. So obviously, it's not realistic or responsible for a court to simply listen to what the child wants and then just go with it, as that in and of itself may not be best for the child.

Admittedly, the information above fails drastically at giving clients a sense of certainty in the process. This happens often with issues in Family Court. But, I have gained some perspective based on my years of experience litigating high-conflict, high-asset divorce and paternity matters.

As a rule of thumb, a child under the age of five is not going to be involved in the process in any way. The judge may order a home study, which involves an expert going to the child's home and evaluating how the parent and child interact, or something to that effect. Maybe in abuse or molestation cases, the court will have an expert engage in play therapy with the child, and observe the child in this particular setting. Sometimes in abuse case, we have a highly trained mental health professional talk to the child. There are other tools we use in Family Court to gather information such as a parenting conference or custody evaluation, obviously depending on the financial resources of the parties. But as a whole, no one is talking to children under five.

When a child is roughly between the age of five and ten, courts will start listening to what they have to say. That said, the court in these instances, has broad discretion about how much weight they are going to give to what they hear. It is widely understood that as children get older, they tend to express their feelings, wishes, and desires more often than they did when they were younger. And they are clearly much less apt to try to appease a parent when they talk about where they want to live. It is considerations such as these that play into the influence a child's statements might have on a judge.

When dealing with 11-15 year olds, the analysis changes a bit, which makes sense. The children in this age range are growing up and becoming more mature. They are beginning to speak for themselves in a thoughtful and educated fashion. So, understandably, what they say weighs more heavily on the judge's mind or on a mental health care provider's recommendation to a judge. In short, the child's wishes are given more weight due to a presumably heightened maturity level.

Now, with respect to 15-17 year olds, the courts can certainly decide and enter particular orders about visitation, but I have heard a judge say more than once, "I can order whatever, but the child is going to do what the child wants to do especially when the child has a driver's license." Because of this reality, I encourage divorcing parents who have children within this age range to carefully evaluate whether taking this issue to court is something they want to spend their money on.

After a child reaches the age of 18 in Arizona, he or she is emancipated by operation of law, and the courts no longer have jurisdiction over the child, and can therefore no longer dictate where they live primarily or which parent they spend time with.

I see this all the time, where, for instance, a sixteen year old daughter hates her mother for whatever reason. They just don't get along, the teenager thinks the mother is overbearing, and they just can't stand each other. Although dad could get primary care over the daughter, mom wants to have equal time and be the primary provider for the daughter. The question I would have is whether it is worth bringing the action to court when, by the time you get to court, the child is almost emancipated?

Let's assume the judge gives the mother what she wants. Is that relationship really going to be healthy? Can you even enforce that order? When it comes to enforcing parenting time, the court expects a parent not to interfere with it, but to facilitate it. At 16 years old, good luck! You do not have an obligation in Arizona to force a child into a car against their will, to go to one parent or the other. Child custody and parenting time with teenage children is better negotiated outside the courtroom if you want a healthy relationship with your children.

YOU AGAIN? PARENTING COORDINATORS TO THE RESCUE!

As a divorce attorney, I represent high-conflict family law, and I've been doing this long enough that I've seen just about everything. I see parents who can't get past their animosity, even 5 or 10 years after their divorce has been finalized. They'll fight about everything you can think of, they're always at each other's throats, and they will refuse to agree with each other out of principle. These people go back to court for everything. Just because you get divorced and there's a divorce decree, that doesn't make the issues of legal decision-making and parenting time final.

For most parents, it is reassuring to know that the issues of legal decision-making and parenting time are always modifiable if a substantial and continuing change of circumstances can be established. To some, however, this could mean endless years of litigation fighting over everything from where a child will go to high school to whether a child can get a tattoo or piercing.

You can tell almost from the moment the Judge takes the bench that he is flat-out sick and tired of seeing a particular pair of litigants fighting over their children. Frankly, some parents just can't seem to move past their own differences for the sake of the children. Other parents just have such different parenting styles that coming to a consensus is out of the question. With the serious risk of being slapped with attorney's fees, or worse yet, damaging their children beyond repair, some parents ultimately make the wise choice to find an alternative to solving their problems.

There are so many issues that affect a child. "Do we put him in kindergarten now or do we hold the child back? Should he go to private school or public school? Which pediatrician should he see?" There are so many issues that arise in a child's life, and some parents can never seem to agree, so they return to court. They're always spending vast amounts of money on their attorneys' fees.

Although I'm happy to represent people in these high-conflict cases, there comes a point when the judge looks at them and says, "It's you again, can't you guys figure it out?" You can tell from the court's ruling from that point forward that they're sick of it. In Arizona, you can be assessed attorney's fees or be ordered to pay the other party's attorney's fees if you're found to be unreasonable. After getting slammed with these attorneys' fees, they may finally say, "I don't want to do this anymore. I don't want to incur the cost and I'm tired of fighting. Is there an alternative?"

When that happens, I will suggest that they might be best served with what's called "the parenting coordination process." It's a very unique process, and it's an extremely efficient way of dealing with issues when parents can't agree on things.

A parenting coordinator could be an attorney, a psychiatrist, a psychologist, social worker, counselor, therapist, or any other certified professional with the appropriate education, experience and expertise related to family law matters.

Parenting coordinators can have a wide variety of backgrounds, training, and experience, and even styles. My job is to help guide clients to choose the right one who is equipped to handle their particular issues. As a divorce attorney I've dealt with them so I can inform and advise clients about their tendencies. It's all part of diligently representing a client, to point them in the direction that may benefit them.

How do you choose a parenting coordinator? You can agree with your attorney's choice or a judge can choose one for you. A judge may not have a firm grasp on your particular family dynamics, so I always encourage clients to work toward on agreeing on the selection of a parenting coordinator and not be difficult about the selection process. It's always better to find somebody who's going to understand your dynamics rather than have a judge impose somebody on you.

The appointments usually last a year, but it is possible to change or remove a PC (parent coordinator) if you have good reason to do so. Once legal decision-making and parenting time orders have been established, these PCs can help deal with almost any issue that affects the child. But they are generally most effective in situations involving persistent conflict as I described earlier, or a history of substance abuse or family violence, mental health issues, or special needs situations.

In the courtroom you have to deal with all its formalities; potential evidence restrictions, limitations of time—all sorts of formal restrictions. PCs don't have these restrictions. They can really roll up their sleeves, get their hands dirty, and investigate the issues fully so that they get to the facts. It's a much quicker process, and less confrontational than other traditional forms of litigation. The fact that it's a much quicker process is attractive to clients. For example, let's say you have to make a decision about your 5 year old born in August, about whether to start the child in kindergarten or hold him back and wait a year. By the time you get to court, the decision has been made for you by the expiration of time. In cases like this, the couples really like the fact that the process with a PC is more expeditious.

Attorneys have fairly limited involvement in the parenting coordination process. You can imagine how not having lawyers involved streamlines and simplifies the process. Each parenting coordinator operates a little differently. Generally, one of the parents reaches out to the PC, and a meeting is scheduled where they try to hash out the issues. Sometimes the PCs will try to get the issue resolved by email or through an informal meeting with both parents.

What's attractive about the process is that there's also a settlement component in addition to the information gathering component. If an agreement is reached, it is committed to writing, signed by both parties, then submitted to the court for approval. The court signs off and it becomes an order. That's the process in a perfect world. However, if there is no agreement, then the parenting coordinator gathers the information, then issues a report and recommendations to the court. Once the report is submitted, each party has 10 days to object to the recommendations and say why they think the recommendation should or should not be adopted by the court. Potentially, there's a hearing on it if the judge says, "I want to hear more," or the judge can decide to adopt the PC's recommendations, modify them, or simply not agree to adopt them.

A PC has broad authority to handle many types of decision-making and parenting time disputes. For example, a PC can assist with the implementation of Court orders, make recommendations to the Court regarding implementation, clarification, modification or enforcement of temporary or even permanent Court orders and make recommendations regarding day-to-day issues. This would include things such as the choice of a child's school, course of medical treatment, parenting time exchanges, holiday parenting time, discipline and extra-curricular activities. That said, there are some limitations on what a PC can do and it is important for clients to understand what those limitations are before heading into the process. For instance, a PC generally cannot address a relocation issue, a change in legal decision-making (e.g. from joint to sole or vice-versa) or a substantial change to the regular access parenting time schedule (e.g. changing from one primary parent to the other). Unfortunately, for these issues, a litigant must still pursue the more traditional method of seeking Court intervention.

This process is growing in popularity in Arizona, and for good reason. It helps people save legal fees, the process is much faster than traditional litigation, and it also unclogs the court system.

WHAT DO WE DO WITH YOUR HOUSE?

A question I receive from virtually every client is, "What do I do with our house?" I relate the question to the TV show, "Love It or List It." Each episode depicts a couple presented with the option of either renovating their existing home and continuing to live there, or purchasing an entirely new home. At the end of the episode, almost without fail, the couple harmoniously agrees on what they want to do, to either "Love It Or List It." Well, that's definitely not the case in divorce cases.

Most divorce cases I run across have at issue, at least one community parcel of real property that must be disposed of in some form or fashion. The analysis starts by taking a look at whether there is equity in the property. In other words, taking a look at the fair market value of the property as compared to any liens or encumbrances that may be attached to the property. Determining value is fairly simple and can be accomplished in a handful of ways. A good starting point is to look at a tax valuation statement or by referencing online resources such as Zillow.com. That said, however, the most reliable methods I've found are having a qualified realtor or real estate agent gather comparable properties (more commonly known as "comps") or having a licensed appraiser perform an appraisal. Most experienced family law attorneys have a rolodex (or iPhone) full of names of experts in these fields to assist in ascertaining an accurate value of a particular home.

Once value is determined, we look at what encumbrances may be associated with the property. This might include a first mortgage, second mortgage, home equity line of credit or tax lien. Performing a search on the county recorder's website is a smart approach to ensuring that all encumbrances associated with the property are identified.

These encumbrances reduce the value of the property and will most certainly need to be satisfied upon any sale. We also take into consideration the fact that the equity in the property may also be reduced by real estate commissions and closing costs if the residence is sold. These factors should all be considered when deciding which position to take in a divorce case.

In a situation where the property may be worth less than is owed, I always recommend that my clients consult with a real estate attorney to discuss options and potential liability. Arizona is an anti-deficiency state, but depending on the type of mortgage(s) associated with the property, a client may have some significant exposure depending on what option they decide to pursue in their divorce. A "short sale" or foreclosure may have serious tax consequences, FICO credit score impacts and even potential financial liability if there is a deficiency (i.e. the house sells at auction for less than is owed on it). The law in this area is ever-changing and an experienced family law attorney can point a client in the right direction.

You can almost bet the farm that if you cannot *agree upon* a disposition of the property with your spouse, your Family Court Judge will order that it be sold. Judges simply do not have the time (or the patience) to get creative. I affectionately refer to this simplistic approach as the "guillotine" method. Sometimes I wonder if some Judges would cut the house in half if they could just to avoid the headache. Perhaps the family has spent the last 20 years in the home and one spouse desperately wants to stay for the stability of the children. This result oftentimes presents a harsh reality for some clients, or perhaps even both parties, which frequently drives settlement discussion on this issue. This is when lawyers step in. I have penned several complicated, convoluted – yet creative and effective- property settlement agreements.

One important thing to remember is that the Family Court does not have proper jurisdiction (authority) to order third-party lenders to do, or not do, anything. This would include forcing the lender to refinance a spouse off a particular mortgage. Prior to 2007, this was not a problem. Most homes had equity, unemployment was low and people for the most part were doing well financially. It was the "good ol' days." Spouses were able to buy-out the other spouse by taking out equity and they were able to refinance the other spouse off the mortgage at the same time without any pushback from the lender. Now things are different. Although the real estate market is rebounding, a large portion of homes are still "upside-down" which limits the divorcing parties' options. Nevertheless, a good attorney can be called upon to come up with creative solutions to solve the epidemic problem. For instance, a spouse can be given some time to refinance to allow for the mortgage to be paid down and for the market to rebound further. Of course, this requires certain safeguards and methods to resolve disputes down the road.

Some divorces take years but parties are not necessarily required to put up with their spouse until the divorce is final. Often one spouse or the other vacates the residence voluntarily once a divorce is looming. However, if both spouses dig in their heels and want to stay in the marital residence, a more formal approach may be necessary. If good cause exists, an Order of Protection (restraining order) is perhaps the swiftest way to oust a spouse from the marital residence. But more commonly, a spouse can file a Motion asking the Court for exclusive use and possession of the residence.

The downside to this approach is that it may take a couple of months to obtain such relief from the Court unless an emergency exists. Interestingly, in the midst of the downturn in the economy, some couples chose to remain living together to preserve community funds. However, when a request is made, it is very likely the Court will order one party to leave. It's easy to understand that problems might arise if divorcing spouses are required to live together under the same roof.

If only it were as easy as having a television network send a realtor and a home designer to your divorce trial to testify, and then you and your spouse deciding which option would benefit the common good. Not shockingly, though, spouses going through a divorce don't see eye to eye. But be warned, if parties can't find a way to swallow their pride and bury their animosity, the result may very well be something neither party can live with.

INSIGHTS INTO RELOCATION

Obviously, when one party moves with their children, it is going to have a significant impact on the other parent's ability to exercise parenting time. If either party decides to relocate, they need to know that there are orders in place regarding legal decision-making and parenting time, and they can't just pack up and leave with the children. A party can certainly move to wherever he or she wants, but the real issue is whether they can take the children with them.

If there is a written agreement or court order for joint legal decision-making, and both parents have unsupervised parenting time, and both parents still reside in the State of Arizona, a relocating parent must first take certain steps to notify the other parent of the intended move. If a relocating parent has sole legal decision-making, and only supervised parenting time is afforded to the other parent, then the relocating parent does not have to provide notice. So, in other words, the non-relocating parent under this latter scenario really has no say in the matter. If you think that's not fair, you're not the only one.

The notice requirement applies to moves outside of Arizona and moves greater than 100 miles within Arizona. For instance, a move across town would not trigger the notice provision (at least not at the moment), but a move from Phoenix to Bullhead City, Arizona or Laughlin, Nevada would. The relocating parent's residence at the time of entry of the existing legal decision-making and parenting time orders is what is used as a starting point for calculating distance.

What does providing notice entail? Well, for starters, the relocating parent is required to send notice to the other parent by certified mail, return receipt requested, or by personally serving the other parent with the notice using a process server. This must be accomplished at least 60 days prior to your anticipated departure date. It is imperative that parties comply with the notice requirements before moving, or they could face serious sanctions, which could include financial penalties, losing decision-making status or worse yet, a significant reduction in parenting time.

Once notice has been properly given, the other parent must file a Petition to Prevent Relocation with the court within 30 days. If a Petition is filed by the non-relocating parent, then a hearing is set, so buckle up. If such a Petition is not timely filed by the non-relocating parent, then the relocating parent is free to go with the children. Keep in mind, though, that only under some rare circumstances is the relocating parent given permission to move prior to the court's determination, so it is not wise to bank on this.

The burden is on the relocating parent to show that relocation is in the children's best interests. The best interest factors can be found in A.R.S. § 25-403, and the court will also apply and weigh several other factors set forth in A.R.S. § 25-408, with an eye toward ensuring a continuation of a meaningful relationship between the children and both parents. Very few relocation requests are granted, and those that are, often involve an expert witness. As can be imagined, these cases can be very expensive to litigate, so it's important to be sure to hire a competent lawyer to assist.

Parties will want to have their ducks in a row before giving notice. Knowing where you will be living, where the children will be going to school, and where you will be working are just a few pieces of the puzzle that are essential to success. Typically, financial considerations are the most important to a Judge and give a litigant the best chance of prevailing. In other words, from what I've experienced, moving because of a better financial opportunity for yourself, or your spouse, gives a party the best shot at being able to move with the children.

Everything seems clear now, right? Well, the law regarding relocation is in flux at the moment and major changes are possibly right around the corner. Things may change in Arizona very soon in light of recent proposed legislative amendments to A.R.S. § 25-408, geared at addressing weaknesses in the current relocation statute. S.B. 1072 is a Bill that was currently passed by the Senate and is being considered by the House of Representatives in Arizona. The proposed change in the law would require all parents, regardless of their decision-making authority or the other parent's parenting time arrangements, to give notice to the other parent of an intended move. Furthermore, perhaps the most significant change is that the statute would apply to *any* move – not just those more than 100 miles away or outside of Arizona. The revised statute would also require relocating parents to provide more specific information in their notice, such as specific language notifying the other parent they have a right to file a Notice of Objection if the move will result in a material change of circumstances affecting the best interests of the child, and providing more detailed information about where they will be moving to and the like.

Arguably, these changes could apply to a parent moving across the street or moving from one apartment to another within the same complex (although moves less than two miles are presumed not to result in a material change). Indeed, my opinion is that the current provisions of the statute are antiquated and require some revision, but unfortunately, the changes as proposed may lead to unintended consequences, such as an influx of cases filed in Arizona courts with already overburdened dockets, constitutional challenges by parents based on the right to travel, and an abuse of the legal system by litigants wishing to re-open previous court orders based on frivolous reasons. These issues have caused a feverish debate amongst legislature and family law practitioners; it will be interesting to see how everything plays out.

ELECTRONIC MEDIA IN A DIVORCE

My number one priority in a divorce case is to protect and preserve my client's confidentiality. Divorce cases can be hotly contested and emotionally-driven, and you see the worst side of people. At times they're willing to do anything, including violating the law on privacy and eavesdropping, to get an advantage, whether it be dealing with financial issues or with the kids. A lot of these cases are driven by infidelity or distrust, and that really drives people to want to cause problems for their spouses.

My goal in representing them is to protect their confidentiality and make sure that we have a secure line of communication. It's my first priority, and it's a crucial element of providing them successful representation and achieving the outcome that they want. The importance of a free flow of information between me and my clients cannot be understated. They need to feel comfortable telling me anything that they want, and not having it come back and bite them. Whether it be drug use, infidelity or hidden accounts, they really need to know that what they talk about is safe.

People want divorce to be private. If they could slink in and slink out of a lawyer's office or the courthouse, they would. This is an embarrassing episode in their lives and they try to keep it from their neighbors, friends, and even family. They certainly don't want their private conversations with their lawyer being dragged into a public forum (the court). It's for these reasons that the first bit of advice I give clients is to change the passwords for all their electronic methods of communication. That would include email accounts and social networking sites.

For people who intend to file a divorce, this should be done as soon as that decision has been made, or as soon as you sense a problem in the relationship, for that matter. As soon as there are problems in a relationship, you need to start locking stuff down. At the very least, start changing the passwords once the other spouse has been served with divorce papers. I always encourage clients to open up a completely new email account to communicate with me, to create a password that is unique, and doesn't include a child's name, a pet's name, or a favorite number, and never, ever, ever set the password to the word 'password.'

I advise my clients to consider using an Internet-based email such as Gmail, Yahoo, or Hotmail, because any email downloaded to your computer will be stored on the computer long after you have deleted it, and it can be recovered by your spouse. Make sure that you password-protect everything: your phone, computer, and any other electronic devices that you may use. Technology's come a long way these days and it's really a big factor in my cases. I can't think of a case in the last three years, that didn't somehow involve Facebook or Twitter. They cause problems in one way or another, whether it be the root of the problem or exacerbation of the problem.

It's important for litigants to understand this: Spyware is easy to find and it's cheap these days. It can be installed on a cell phone, tablet, or notebooks in a few minutes, when you're taking a shower or going to the grocery store. Spyware can capture keyboard logging, duplicate emails to another mailbox, capture screenshots, GPS devices, even LoJack, in the car. You can also access the GPS devices on the cell phone and your vehicle. This is some of the spyware tracking technology that people use to attain incriminating information about their spouses, and some of this technology is easy to install. Spyware is so sophisticated that it takes a forensic expert to determine whether something has been installed on your computer, cell phone or other electronic device, so at a minimum, you should purchase anti-spyware software.

It's wise to periodically review your computer and other devices even after your divorce to ensure your privacy. People sometimes have a gut instinct about these things. If your phone is acting up, your cell phone is slower, the computer is acting funny, or you're getting weird emails, or if you're tipped off or you have a suspicion, go with your gut. Think about hiring a forensic expert to go through your computer and scour through your files for spyware.

As far as social network sites go, I can't tell you how frequently I come across Facebook posts which contain incriminating, or at the very least, embarrassing content. And why is this important? This stuff can be used to support a waste claim. If you go on a ski trip with your mistress and you post something about the trip, and it's supported by a bank statement that shows you spent $1,000 at the resort, that can form a basis for a waste claim. Also, this type of evidence can establish unfitness of a parent as it relates to parenting time.

In Arizona, the word 'waste' is found nowhere in the statutes, but it's a case-law-derived claim where if the spouse uses community money, not for a community purpose, and it's somehow wasteful, then the other spouse can have a claim for reimbursement. If community money was earned during the marriage, your spouse has the right to half of it. If one spouse uses that money to pay for a diamond ring for his mistress, there's a possible claim there. That's a waste claim.

People try to get information from emails, Facebook, and other social networking sites to support their waste claims, parenting time positions, and allegations about fitness. Arizona is a no-fault divorce state. In other words, no fault has to be established to obtain a divorce, so proving infidelity in and of itself is not particularly persuasive to a judge. Although infidelity is not persuasive to a court, these waste issues and parenting time concerns are. So don't think that just because Arizona is a no-fault state, you don't need to worry about infidelity, because it can be relevant. My advice to clients is to at least keep social media postings to a minimum, especially during the divorce.

This applies even after you are divorced, because modifications can happen to the legal decision-making and parenting time. Five years down the road, you don't want all the postings that you put on Facebook to be used against you. Remove any mutual friends from your social network page, because that could give your spouse/ex-spouse an entry into your personal posts. Think about how information makes you look when you post something on Facebook, and how other people will perceive you if they see what you have posted. I could almost guarantee that your spouse/ex-spouse is watching and will use it against you. If you must have a page, set it to private. Also, change your passwords frequently.

The privacy issue varies between jurisdictions and there are even some federal law implications that could have serious consequences for your freedom and your pocketbook. There are some distinctions in the law, from jurisdiction to jurisdiction, and in the Federal Law, that revolve around whether the communication has already been stored, like emails; or whether the communication is intercepted in transmission, like recording a phone conversation, for instance.

The contemporaneousness of the transmission is important with regard to computers, emails, and social media sites, also the location of the device on which the information is stored or transmitted. It is relevant where the computer or device is located - in your office upstairs, a general office, or your home office. The court will want to know if both of you historically have used that computer, who has access to it generally, and whether the computer, Facebook account, or Twitter account, is password-protected. These are all crucial issues.

With regard to tapping somebody's communication, generally in Arizona, if you're a party to the conversation, then you can tape it. If I have a client who says, "I want to tape the conversation with my husband," that's generally fine. But eavesdropping, or wire-tapping, typically on conversations that you're not a party to could get you into some serious trouble.

It could have an impact on the court's decision regarding legal decision-making and parenting time. My nugget of advice for this would be to talk to your divorce lawyer about these issues before, not after, because once you do it, if it's wrong, you're in trouble. Then you have put your lawyer in a really tough jam in terms of whether he or she can continue representing you. Talk to your lawyer before taking any steps to subversively obtain information about your spouse for purposes of using it in a lawsuit. You could be opening yourself up to charges of invasion of privacy, trespassing the channels, theft, or conversion, which have associated criminal penalties.

DEATH TO THE FIRST RIGHT OF REFUSAL

I discuss the term "first right of refusal" with potential clients when I first sit down with them for an initial consultation. When I ask them if they have ever heard of the term, and know what the term means, they usually stare back at me with a bewildered, blank look on their faces. I later find out they understand the concept, and may have even had similar issues with their spouse, but simply did not know there was an actual name for it.

This concept has been around since I can remember. Although you won't find the term specifically mentioned in any statute or rule here in Arizona, parties are free to agree to such a provision, and Judges have historically issued such an order if a compelling reason can be established.

When a parent is unable to provide care for their children during their regularly scheduled parenting time, for whatever reason, the first right of refusal requires that parent to contact the other parent first before making alternative care arrangements. Common reasons for a parent to be unavailable include travel out of town for work, having to work late and scheduled events at which it would not be appropriate for the children to attend. I will also often hear a client complain their former spouse is going out on the weekend with friends and leaving the children with someone else.

The new spouse or the new person in the other party's life will never be perceived as being as good as they are, and there's always some animosity there. So there may be a concern about leaving the kids with that person while the parent goes off on a business trip, golf outing or fishing trip. This provision does not apply when the kids are at school, when the children are at extra-curricular activities, during normal work hours for a parent, or when the parent is on vacation with the children.

If it seems a divorcing couple is open to the suggestion of incorporating a first right of refusal provision into their Parenting Plan, the discussion then centers on exactly how much time the parent must be unavailable before the right of refusal is triggered. It can be two hours, four hours or even 24 hours. A parent's confidence or comfort level in the other parent's judgment about choosing alternative care providers typically dictates the length of time.

In order to prevent future conflict, it is also prudent to have at least a preliminary discussion about who a parent intends to use as an alternative care provider so that any issues can be vetted. I insist on an order that each parent be required to disclose to the other parent the names of roommates, friends, significant others and any other individuals who will be spending significant time around the children. And I further encourage clients to run a thorough background check on these people. You hear news stories every day about the awful things that people are doing to innocent children. You hear news stories almost every day about kids being harmed by step-parents.

These children are being murdered, beaten or kidnapped. You can never be too safe these days!

It is important to make sure that clients understand and recognize that a clear and concise parenting time schedule is implemented so that both parents and the children have knowledge of, will be able to look forward to, and will be able to plan their respective schedule, including free time for the parents, based on the schedule. This is why we do parenting plans. That said, even though the offer must be extended by the unavailable parent, the other parent is in no way obligated to exercise the right of first refusal. In other words, the unavailable parent should not rely upon or assume the other parent will pick up the slack at their beck and call. If the right is not elected, then the unavailable parent is the one responsible for finding alternative care arrangements. It's that parent's responsibility, (the parent who has the parenting time), to find alternative care, whether that means a babysitter, another family member, or a friend. Most parents are happy to have more parenting time, and will say, "Absolutely. I'd love to see them more."

You might ask what happens in a situation when a parent elects the right but then that parent is unavailable for more than the designated period of time. Well, if not addressed by the parties' parenting plan, then who knows. This is just one example of when a first right of refusal provision does more harm than good. There are many others and it is impossible to foresee them all.

One problem with a first right of refusal is if you don't trust the other parent, then you're forced into a situation of interrogating the children, to find out whether that parent has been gone for more than two hours, or whatever the specified time is. You're not there to know whether the person is complying with this order, so you're asking the kids, "Hey, was Dad ever gone for a period of two hours or more?" This is just one of the reasons that the courts in Arizona are moving towards doing away with this provision. More often than not, judges don't even bring it up. If it's brought up, you'll find judges who won't order it. If the parties agree, and want this provision, the court will adopt it, but if you leave it up to a judge, you're probably not going to get the provision because of this conflict.

These parties and litigants are coming back to them over and over again talking about this issue, and I've had many judges tell me that this provision's caused more harm than good. They'd rather have the parties just find an alternative care provider. Ideally, one hopes that the parent will call the other parent, but they're not required to. I've seen examples where doing away with first right of refusal, actually encourages the parents to call the other parent more, because they don't have to. Furthermore, you can always have the grandparents watch them. Judges want grandparents to remain involved as much as possible, and not being required to call the other parent provides an opportunity for other family members to provide care, thereby developing stronger family relationships.

I have noticed Judges more openly discourage the practice of including such provisions in parenting plans. In a world where conflict is rampant, sometimes it behooves even the most seasoned family attorney to take a step back, put habit aside and figure out whether the first right of refusal is something that truly benefits their client in the long run.

(This content should be used for informational purposes only. It does not create an attorney-client relationship with any reader and should not be construed as legal advice. If you need legal advice, please contact an attorney in your community who can assess the specifics of your situation.)

Alexandra M. White
Law Office of Alexandra White PC
Centennial, CO

Alex developed a passion for family law while serving as a Group Facilitator with the Kids First program in Honolulu, a program designed for parents and children experiencing divorce. She understands that in cases where children are involved, their needs are paramount. She has experience handling cases where children's lives are affected by complex adult issues such as substance abuse and domestic violence.

PSYCHOLOGICAL CONSIDERATIONS

Divorce is a very emotional event in life and that is expected and normal. The outcome of a divorce can vary according to your goals. I think a post-divorce goal should be to place yourself in a position where you can move on with your life and have what you need.

If your goal is to be vindicated, that may not happen. What the judge looks at is not whether someone deserves to be punished but the financial circumstances in terms of what you're entitled to, what you need, and a fair resolution of the financial issues that you have. In the end, the judgment may very well vindicate you, but it may not—and you need to be prepared for that. Hopefully, it puts you in a place where you can recover from the divorce and move on with your life.

THE DIVORCE PROCESS

A divorce is a multi-step dispute resolution process. The mechanics of initiating a divorce depend on the state in which you're located. In the State of Colorado, a document called the Petition for Dissolution of Marriage is prepared and is served on the other party. The Petition is a very basic document that identifies you, your spouse, and your children as well as informing the court of the basic areas of dispute (for example, maintenance).

There are a couple of different ways you can serve your spouse. You can either serve your spouse using a process server, or you can do things in a more amicable way, perhaps by sitting down with your spouse and telling him or her that you've made the decision to file for divorce, and then asking him or her to sign the document (he or she will still need to sign the document before a notary public).

The next step is to decide the process you wish to use to get divorced. A divorce is considered a dispute, and there are several ways to resolve a dispute. One is through litigation. Litigation is a dispute resolution process that takes place in a courtroom in front of a judge with or without an attorney. There are alternatives to dispute resolution through the court system. Some parties choose to participate in arbitration, which is a dispute resolution alternative that is binding for the parties. In other words, the arbitration process allows a third party to make a binding decision regarding the disputes between the parties. Participants in an arbitration proceeding often agree to proceed in a more informal manner than they would in a courtroom. The arbitration process can be as formal as a courtroom setting or as informal as an office or conference room setting. Mediation is another route to resolving divorce issues, but mediation is not a binding process. In other words, the mediator cannot issue a binding decision. Mediation is required by courts in Colorado before the judge will hear your case. However, parties can mediate their issues before the divorce (litigation) process is even started.

In our state as well as in many other states, there is another alternative to litigation which is called the collaborative law process. Parties can decide to engage in the collaborative law process at any time during the divorce process. It can start in the middle of the proceedings or, preferably, before a divorce is started. The collaborative law process is initiated with the hope that the parties will be able to resolve their differences not only outside of a courtroom but in a healing environment that attempts to addresses all of the conflicts between the parties—not just the conflicts that judges view as important.

When children are involved, divorce becomes more complex. Like financial issues, children's issues are mediated or resolved either in litigation or in an alternative dispute resolution process. I think that, generally speaking—whether it's about parenting time or financial matters—reaching a resolution outside of the courtroom is a better approach for both parties because they control the outcome of their divorce. When disputes are resolved by a judge, the process is adversarial and you are allowing a third party, a judge whom you don't know, to resolve your disputes. Very often, the outcome in a courtroom setting is not pleasing to either party. Settling your case, whether through collaborative law, mediation, or negotiations through attorneys, gives you more control over how you will resolve your disputes. Instead of subjecting yourself to a decision that you may or may not like, you understand and take ownership of the dispute resolution. Usually, the outcome is better for everyone involved if an agreement can be reached outside a courtroom on disputed issues.

Child support and visitation (which is called parenting time in Colorado) are interrelated in Colorado. The amount of child support a parent pays is highly affected by the number of overnights he or she has with the children. Simply put, more time spent with the children reduces the amount of the support obligation to the other parent. That may give parties an incentive to push for more time with the children even if they believe that it would be in the children's best interest to spend more time with the other parent. Unfortunately, the information we can provide to the judge in a courtroom is very restricted by the rules of evidence. If there is no mental health professional present, the judge often will lack crucial information about the children and the dynamics of the family—information that the judge would need in order to accurately determine whether a parent is manipulating.

Sometimes the best way to prevent this type of manipulation is to employ a mental health professional or evaluator. In Colorado, this professional is a called a Child & Family Investigator (CFI) or Parental Responsibility Evaluator (PRE). Employing a CFI or PRE who can testify about the children and the family dynamics may be the only way your judge will actually get to know your family. In the absence of one of these professionals, the court may not know that a parent is pushing for more time with the kids for financial reasons. Furthermore, the court won't necessarily know that the best interest of the children involves spending more time with the other parent.

It's important for each parent to look closely at why he or she is fighting about parenting time and question whether or not the fight is really about the kids.

As mentioned above, mediation is an alternative method to resolving child custody and support issues. The process of mediation does not automatically bring in a CFI or PRE. In addition, parties generally can choose to mediate their case either before or after an investigator completes his or her investigation. Often, if parties are unsuccessful mediating children's issues initially, they will mediate again after an investigation is completed when more information is known. The flow of information in mediation is not restricted like it is in a courtroom setting. The parties can tell the mediator things that a court would not be able to hear unless the judge was hearing the information from a CFI or PRE (such as something one of the children said, for example). An evaluative mediator will give the parties his or her opinion of what might happen if a judge hears their case, which stimulates settlement discussion.

The mediator will hear both sides of the story and both parties' perception of what is in the best interest of the children. If a report has already been issued by a CFI or PRE, it is useful to allow the mediator to review the report prior to mediation. Deciding whether to mediate before or after a report is completed often comes down to the resources of the parties—an evaluation can cost between $2,000 to $25,000 (or more, in some cases), so if the parties can resolve their differences without a report, it is worth a try.

INSIGHTS INTO POST-DIVORCE ISSUES

Some people think that once they get their final divorce judgment, that's the end of it. Unfortunately for some, post-divorce issues arise all the time and these can require a modification to your divorce judgment.

There are several ways to process post-divorce issues. Some people agree at the end of their divorce to sit down with a mediator and try to resolve disputes before anyone files any motions with the court. In this scenario, a post-decree process is begun simply by one party asking the other party to participate in mediation. If an agreement is reached, it's always recommended that they put that agreement in writing and file it with the court. If they can't reach an agreement, the next step is to file a motion with the court which will trigger the start of a post-decree proceeding; much as filing a petition for dissolution of marriage starts the divorce process.

There are several issues that may arise post-divorce. Child support is always modifiable, and parenting time is always modifiable. In some circumstances, maintenance (called alimony in some states) is modifiable. Maintenance is not modifiable if, at the time the divorce decree was entered, the parties agreed that the court does not have jurisdiction to modify maintenance in the future. Absent extraordinary circumstances, the terms of the property division are not modifiable. Any order that is child-related is going to be modifiable until the children are emancipated.

If someone wants to ask for a modification, there must be a valid reason. There's a requirement that parties have to meet in order to ask for a change in the orders. For each issue, there is a different standard that the person has to assert to the court in order to seek a modification of the order. For example, a party seeking a modification of child support in Colorado has to at least assert in the motion they file that they believe there has been a substantial and continuing change of circumstances such that a modification of child support is warranted. Ultimately, whether or not a substantial and continuing change of circumstances has actually occurred will be determined by the judge. If the application of Colorado's child support guidelines to the parties' current financial circumstances results in a 10% increase or decrease in the child support obligation, the judge will likely find that a substantial change of circumstances has occurred.

On parenting time, the standard is different, depending on the kind of change that the person is seeking. If a person is asking for a shift in parenting time that doesn't change the children's primary residence, the standard is that they believe a modification of parenting time would be in the best interest of the children. If the party is asking for a change in primary residential care, then there is a higher standard because research shows that a change in primary residential care can be destructive to a child's development. This kind of change is certainly necessary at times, but the value must outweigh the harm. So the parent seeking to change the primary caretaker has to assert that the children will be endangered unless the change occurs. There are some exceptions to this standard, such as the relocation of a parent.

Agreeing on a change in any court order is almost always better for everyone involved than going to court. However, it is always advisable for people to reduce their agreements to writing and even file the agreement with the Court. Many people make changes to their parenting schedule after a divorce is over and never return to court. Some of these people do just fine. The interrelationship between parenting time and child support often causes people to formalize their agreements when a substantial parenting time change is implemented. If they shift the overnights from one party to another, that may change (or create) a child support obligation. However, if the shift doesn't affect the number of overnights allocated to the parents, and neither parent is asking for a change in child support, many people don't put the change in writing.

When the relationship between parents is highly adversarial, reducing agreements to writing and filing the agreement with the Court is highly recommended.

INSIGHTS INTO POST-DIVORCE ENFORCEMENT

There are different mechanisms for enforcement of court orders. As with everything in the law, different rules apply depending on the type of enforcement someone is seeking and the type of order that the party is seeking to enforce. For example, there is a whole set of laws and remedies (mechanisms) that are specific to the enforcement of child support or maintenance obligations.

In Colorado, when a party disobeys a court order, the other party can initiate contempt proceedings. Contempt proceedings can be initiated when a party violates virtually any type of order, whether the order requires a party to do something (and the party did not) or the order prohibits a party from doing something (and the party did it anyway). In a contempt proceeding, the party can ask the court to issue sanctions against the other party for disobeying an order. A sanction issued by a court is a punishment for disobeying the court order. Depending on the circumstances, sanctions can include an award of attorneys' fees and costs, imprisonment, or payment of a fine to the court. In Colorado, if the order the party disobeyed was a parenting time order, additional sanctions can include make-up parenting time for the party who lost time, an order modifying parenting time, and even an order that the parties engage in family therapy.

There are additional options available for the enforcement of a family support obligation. In Colorado, there is a higher interest rate that is applied to child support arrears. In addition, each state offers a Child Support Enforcement Agency (a governmental agency) which has power that private attorneys don't have. For example, a state child support enforcement agency has the ability to revoke the obligor's driver's license and/or intercept the obligor's tax refund. Sometimes, a state child support enforcement agency will initiate its own contempt proceedings against an obligor.

In addition to contempt proceedings, a party who is owed money by court order (whether child support, maintenance, or money from a property settlement), he or she can seek a judgment from the Court. The judgment will include interest in most cases. In Colorado, in the absence of an agreement stating otherwise, statutory interest is 8% compounded annually. Interest on child support arrears in Colorado is 12% compounded monthly. Once the Court enters a judgment for an unpaid obligation, that judgment can be recorded and used to place a lien on the obligor's real or personal property.

To illustrate, let's say Joe owes Sally child support. Sally can initiate contempt proceedings against Joe and ask for sanctions. In addition to that, she can seek the entry of a support judgment, which upon filing is automatically entered, and she is entitled to 12% interest compounded monthly (in Colorado). If she's trying to enforce a property division though, her options are a little different. She can still initiate contempt proceedings. She can still seek a judgment (although the judgment is not entered automatically like a support judgment would be) and she would only be entitled to 8% interest compounded annually. For example, let's just say Joe owned a business worth $200,000 at the time of the divorce. Since he was awarded the business, he was ordered to pay her $100,000 (representing her share of the business). If he doesn't pay as ordered, she can enforce that obligation to pay $100,000 by seeking a judgment and initiating contempt proceedings but the state child support enforcement agency won't help Sally and she would not get 12% interest compounded monthly.

With the fluctuations in the housing market, there are people who want to modify their property division because the value of the house they were awarded by the court plummeted after the divorce. For example, at the time of the divorce, Sally wanted to keep the house and the Court awarded it to her. At the time of the divorce the house was valued at $500,000 so Sally was ordered to pay Joe $250,000 for the value of his share of the home. However, one year after the divorce, the value of the home plummeted to $300,000. Even though this seems very unfair, absent extraordinary circumstances, the court will not modify the divorce decree. Sally still has to pay Joe $250,000 for home that is now only worth $300,000. The person who keeps an asset, whether it's a house or a business, must understand that there is a risk of that asset changing in value. That change could be good or bad. The business Joe kept could increase from $200,000 to $800,000 in one year; but Sally cannot go back to court and ask for more money for her portion of the business (absent extraordinary circumstances or unless Sally can prove that Joe didn't disclose information at the time of the divorce which would have allowed her to know or have reason to know that the business was worth more).

PSYCHOLOGICAL CONSIDERATIONS OF GETTING A DIVORCE

Every divorce carries with it psychological consequences. For most people who go through a divorce, it is a pretty traumatic event. It can be traumatizing for the husband and the wife and also for the children. Hopefully, the divorce process will result in healing, especially where children are involved. Healing is more likely to be achieved by the parties reaching resolution of their disputes outside of litigation. Although the parents are divorcing each other, they are not divorcing their children. They continue to be the parents of their children until the children are emancipated, and in reality, all of their lives, so if parents can achieve healing during the divorce process, that is always the best outcome for the kids. Children are incredibly perceptive to their parents' emotions, even though they may not realize it. They pick up on the antagonism and conflict that often comes with a divorce. As parents limit the conflict between themselves, their children will be less likely to experience negative effects of the divorce.

Many people do not realize that the both parents actually might be better parents when the divorce is over. They may stay in a marriage thinking that this is the best thing for their children. But when parents are unhappily married, they spend a lot of their time and emotional energy resolving or attempting to resolve their own conflicts. When that conflict is eliminated, parties often have more emotional capacity to focus on their individual relationships with the children. Similarly, children who are exposed to the conflict between their parents are often relieved when the divorce is over (or even initiated), because there is hope that they will not have to listen to their parents fight anymore. While many parents stay married because they think that it is the best thing for their children (and sometimes it is), they also have to realize that a divorce will protect the children from having to continue to experience the fighting between the parents. Our children also want to see their parents happy. It makes them sad to see their parents sad.

When contemplating a divorce, all of the pros and cons need to be considered. Although divorce can be a very difficult event for everyone involved, in the end, when all of the issues are resolved, the family as a unit can experience healing because parents are better able to devote their emotional energy to their children.

As an attorney, I try to help people understand that my role is to help them resolve their financial and parenting disputes in a legal setting. I have five kids and lots of funny stories to share. I'm divorced but I was also married to my husband and father of my children for 17 years. I've got stories that will make you cry, laugh, scream, and sit on the edge of your chair. But if you have a medical need, you would not come to me for a prescription.

Although every family law attorney needs to have empathy, patience, and the ability to listen, it's important for our clients to realize that we are not therapists. Seeking help from a therapist, personal trainer, or somebody else trained to help you cope with the emotional upheaval of your divorce is better (and more cost effective!) than asking an attorney. When you have an infection, you go to a medical doctor. If you are overweight and want to get trim, you go to a nutritionist and/or a personal trainer. When you are resolving legal issues you hire a lawyer. Find the right professional to "treat" your needs. Doing so can significantly affect the success of the divorce process.

There are various ways to get help and heal emotionally—before, during, and after a divorce. Each person's individual needs are different, and each person copes with emotional stress in different ways. For emotional and psychological help, seeking therapy is highly recommended—even if the sole purpose of that therapy is to determine the coping mechanism that is best suited to you. Sally may benefit the most by attending regular therapy sessions. Joe may achieve more benefit by getting into a workout routine and becoming healthier. Whatever path you need to take to get through the emotional upheaval of the divorce, get on it and take one step at a time.

HIRING THE RIGHT DIVORCE ATTORNEY

It is important for you and your attorney to be in sync concerning style and your desired outcome. Each attorney has a different style, and it's important for the client to be able to identify the type of style that he or she can relate to and desires. Part of that is identifying your goal. Some people—let's name this client Louise—want vindication (perhaps for her own emotional healing). She wants her day in court, and she wants an adversarial attorney. Another client—let's call this client Samantha—is in a different place emotionally. She has children with her husband and her goal is to do the least damage to the parental relationship as a whole, even if that means she gets less money out of the divorce than perhaps she could have. She's interested in collaborative law. Samantha and Louise will most likely pick different lawyers. In a successful attorney–client relationship, there will be harmony.

As a divorce attorney, I am comfortable litigating a case when a case needs to be litigated. In fact, I enjoy a good trial. There are certain cases when the litigation route is the best and only way to resolve a dispute. However, I believe that the best outcome (emotionally and otherwise) is usually reached when the parties are able to resolve their disputes in a manner they direct and control. Therefore, my approach is to facilitate resolution outside of the courtroom whenever possible.

(This content should be used for informational purposes only. It does not create an attorney-client relationship with any reader and should not be construed as legal advice. If you need legal advice, please contact an attorney in your community who can assess the specifics of your situation.)

Sam R. Assini
Men's Rights Law Firm
Cape Coral, FL

Sam Assini is passionate about Men's Rights, aggressively representing the interests of husbands and fathers involved in divorce and other family law matters. Having "been there" himself, he empathizes and understands what men go through and that your case is one of the most important events in your life. Often, divorce settlements leave men feeling like they are "intruders", "visitors" and/or "part-time" parents when, in fact, they are an integral part of the lives as well as the developmental stages of their children.

MEN'S RIGHTS

In order to obtain a divorce in the state of Florida, you must first meet the residency requirement, for the court to have jurisdiction over your case. Under the current law in Florida, the husband and/or wife must have been a resident of the state of Florida for six consecutive months immediately prior to the filing of the case. If the parties are out of the state on a temporary basis but with the intention of returning to Florida, there are limited exceptions, in which the time spent out of state may be counted for the calculation of the six-month residency period. Examples of temporary absences that would be included in the calculation of the six-month period include out-of-state vacations, temporary employment and military service. Once the six-month time period has lapsed, the party may file the action upon his or her return to Florida or from the state in which he or she is temporarily located. For individuals who relocate to Florida from another state, they cannot file for divorce as residents of Florida until they have been living in the state for a minimum of six months.

When a client, let us assume it is the husband, comes to me and expresses that his marriage is irrevocably broken and he wants to dissolve the marriage, I advise him that there are two options to consider. He can either seek a pre-suit uncontested divorce or file a contested divorce action. In a pre-suit uncontested divorce, I discuss issues with my client that must be settled in the divorce, such as issues pertaining to the children (i.e. physical custody, a parenting plan, timesharing, child support, etc.); the division of assets and liabilities; the payment or non-payment of spousal support; payment of attorney fees and costs; and, a name change for the wife if she plans to resume the use of her maiden name. These terms are then incorporated into a marital settlement agreement. The husband must then complete a financial affidavit detailing his assets and liabilities, including any marital assets and liabilities.

After my client has completed his financial affidavit, I then send the proposed marital settlement agreement, my client's financial affidavit, a blank financial affidavit and a letter to the wife explaining to her that we only represent her husband, that signing this agreement will affect her rights and that she should consult with an attorney of her choosing before signing any documents. If the terms of the agreement are acceptable to the wife, she can complete the financial affidavit, sign the agreement with or without consulting an attorney, and return those to my office. After reviewing the wife's financial affidavit with my client, if he agrees with her disclosure, he will sign the marital settlement agreement as well. Once the agreement has been fully executed by both parties, it will be filed with the court along with the financial affidavits of both spouses, an uncontested petition for divorce, answer and waiver. After a twenty-day waiting period expires, the court will enter a final judgment of divorce and the parties are officially divorced. The final judgment is filed with the clerk of court and copies mailed to both parties.

If the parties cannot agree to an uncontested divorce, I must file a petition for dissolution of marriage and related documents with the clerk of court and request a summons be issued to begin a contested divorce proceeding. A process server will serve copies of the summons, petition and all filed documents on the wife. My firm prefers to use a private process server to serve the documents on the other spouse rather than a county sheriff's officer, because it is less upsetting to the spouse and any children who might be present when their parent is served with divorce papers. It can be difficult to explain to children why the police came to their home, or they may assume that their parent is in some type of trouble with the police. We feel it is not a good way to begin the process, so we prefer to use a private process server.

A certificate of service will be filed with the clerk of court to affirm that the spouse has been served and that her twenty-day period to answer and file a counter petition has begun. If she does not file an answer or other responsive pleading within twenty days from the date of service, a default will be entered by the clerk of court. We would then submit a request that a default trial be scheduled for a future date. We serve notice of the final hearing on the wife and she may attend the hearing if she so chooses, but is not required to attend. If the wife chooses to file an answer, counter petition or other responsive pleading, the matter will be litigated.

In an uncontested divorce, full financial disclosure is required by both parties. Both parties will then begin the discovery process by filing and serving requests for documents and other personal information on each other. Additionally, in some cases there will be a need for the filing of motions for the appointment of experts. Because each case is unique, the use of experts varies from case to case. For example, one case may warrant the need for a financial expert while yet another case may require a parenting evaluator or an occupational expert. I have some cases that warrant the use of more than one type of expert. Any experts who are retained to work on the case will perform a full investigation and provide a report and recommendation to the court. The report can be used at future hearings and at the trial of the case.

Examples of where I might utilize an expert include using an occupational expert if the other spouse is unemployed or claiming some type of disability. A financial expert might be employed if the parties own a family business. The occupational expert would consider the wife's education and work history and opine as to what type of employment she is suited for and the jobs that are available in the local community. In the instance of a family business, I would need the financial expert to review the books and other pertinent financial information for the business to determine the proper value for that particular business. In many cases, the family has used funds from the business for personal use; therefore, those funds would need to be included as personal income rather than expenditures of the company. Examples might include gas for personal use, personal car payments, personal entertainment, home mortgage payments and vacations. These additional personal funds would be added to the parties' gross income in their financial affidavits and can be considered when awarding alimony, child support or attorney's fees and costs.

Upon the completion of the discovery phase, mandatory mediation will be scheduled. The mediator is an independent third party who will attempt to help the parties reach an amicable settlement of all outstanding issues. Mediation is a time for the parties to discuss all issues and determine the best way to resolve each in the best interest of the family as a whole. The mediation will usually begin with the discussion of parental responsibility, and then move on to discussing a timesharing schedule, as well as developing a parenting plan for the children. We then move on to a detailed evaluation of the parties' finances, including their assets and their liabilities. Those are equitably divided between the parties. Next the need for alimony will be considered, which affords support to one spouse if needed, but the other spouse has to have the financial ability to pay. The next issue would be the calculation of child support, based upon the Florida Child Support Guidelines. Both parents have a financial responsibility to support their children and are required to pay for health insurance if reasonably available, as well as day care or after school care if necessary. The party who owes a higher financial duty of support based on the guidelines will pay that amount specified in the guidelines to the other spouse. Lastly, attorney's fees and costs are discussed, based on the parties' relevant need and ability to pay, and the restoration of the wife's maiden name if she so wishes.

Because each case is different, mediation may work to resolve all of the issues, some of the issues, or none of the issues. If the parties can come to an agreement on all issues, a fully executed written agreement is filed with the clerk and a final judgment entered by the court that adopts the parties' mediated agreement. Once the final judgment is entered and sent to the parties, they are officially divorced. However, there are cases where mediation does not settle all of the issues. In those cases, the remaining issues, or all issues if none were resolved during mediation, will be tried before the judge assigned to the case.

In this instance, one of the attorneys will request that the case be set for trial, and notice will be sent by the court scheduling a docket sounding so that a date can be assigned for the trial of the case. At the trial, the parties and all witnesses they may have will testify as to the issues before the court. After the presentation of all testimony and evidence, and arguments presented by both attorneys, the judge will pronounce his ruling or take the case under advisement and issue a final judgment at a later date. It all depends on the judge's caseload as to how long the parties will have to wait to receive the judgment. It could take a couple of weeks or even several months in a complicated case. There are some cases in which the judge may order one of the attorneys to prepare the final judgment. In those cases, one attorney will prepare the judgment and send it to opposing counsel for approval. Once both attorneys agree on a final draft that is in accordance with the court's pronouncement, the order is forwarded to the court for entry. If the judge is satisfied as to the form and content of the proposed judgment, he will sign it and the clerk of court will enter it into record. The judgment will then be mailed to the attorneys for distribution to their respective clients.

INSIGHTS INTO FATHER'S RIGHTS

Fathers are now being placed on a more equal playing field with regard to their rights to parent their children. In 2008, the Florida legislature enacted laws regarding timesharing and parenting plans. During the 1800s, children were considered property; therefore, during a divorce the father received custody of the children. It is important to remember that during this period, in an agrarian society, children began working in the fields with their fathers at an early age. The mothers remained home performing other duties such as cooking, cleaning and other household chores.

With the beginning of the Industrial Revolution, fathers left the farm and went to work in factories. Mothers became the primary caregivers of the children during the day. At that time, the legislature enacted the Tender Years Doctrine. Children under the age of eight at the time of the divorce were placed in the custody of the mother unless placing the child with her would be detrimental to the children. Around the time of World War II, the "Rosie-the-Riveter" era, a large percentage of men of child bearing age went to war and women were forced to seek employment in factories.

During the late 1950s and early 1960s, the country saw the birth of the Women's Rights Movement. The "tender years", the age at which a child was automatically placed in the mother's custody, was reduced from eight years to six years, then four and then to two. Eventually the tender years doctrine was abolished in the 1980s. This was about the time that men were getting more involved in raising their children. The woman's loss of these precious rights was an unintended consequence of the women's movement. Women wanted equal rights and received them, but by doing so the door for equal protection arguments based on gender equality argued by men forced the courts and the legislature to enact laws that were gender-neutral in regards to both parents' rights to raise their children.

Men continually fought for equality during these decades of change. Fathers accepted the responsibilities of child rearing and eventually began gaining custody of their children. This abrupt change in the law caused women to reevaluate their stature in the lives of the children. A great deal of litigation ensued as women found it hard to explain how the fathers were gaining custody as well as filling the role of "caretaker" to their children. Some women were shunned or ridiculed by others and seen as "unfit" because they did not receive custody of their children. Society believed that it was always in the best interest of the children to remain in the custody of their mothers unless there was some valid impairment that prevented the mother from properly parenting the children.

The mindset of society continues to change and it has become more acceptable for men to gain custody of their children or become stay-at-home dads as mothers began filling the role of breadwinner for the family. Today, over sixty percent of the students in law school and medical school are women. Although the legislature is slowly catching up to these societal changes, judges seem to remain behind the curve in their attempt to apply the ever-changing custody laws. It is difficult to change "norms" and the prejudices in the minds of some people. Fathers were suddenly performing all the tasks that were thought of as "the mother's job." They changed diapers, fed bottles of formula, and attended school parent-teacher meetings, as well as medical checkups and other appointments. Women would breastfeed in order to keep fathers from partaking in that particular task. They thought that was one arena where they could not be replaced; therefore; that guaranteed them custody of the child. However, with the advent of breast pumps, women can supply ample milk in these situations so that the men can continue feeding while the mother goes off to work. As the father's role as a major caregiver of children has continued to become more prevalent and accepted by society, most people believe that either parent can adequately provide the needed care for children.

It was a big win for fathers when the Florida legislature abolished the term "visitation" from the statutes regarding children as well as the term "custody." Visitation is a term most people think of in relation to visiting an inmate in prison. There was much litigation over which parent should receive physical custody of the children after the Tender Years Doctrine was abolished. Visitation was usually limited so that fathers only saw their children every other weekend for a few hours or at best the entire weekend. Even with the change in the law, there is still a negative stigma associated with a woman who is not granted physical custody of the children or who has to share custody of the children with the father. Some women continue with the old mindset and feel they are "entitled" to custody simply because they are the "mother".

Society has not considered the impact of this custodial arrangement on the children. In most families, the father is the disciplinarian. Fathers are involved in extra-curricular activities and sometimes act as coach of their children's teams. After a divorce, women continue to play the role of nurturer and caregiver of the children; however, they are reluctant to take on the role of disciplinarian. This has caused many of the problems that society faces today with our wayward children. The important role that the father plays in the family has been discounted. The only use society had for the father during a divorce was getting into his deep pockets for money. Society was more interested in getting as much money from "Dad" as possible but society did not have the forethought to consider the consequences of losing the male role model in the lives of our children. The detrimental effect on our children can be seen in all aspects of our society today.

The younger generation is now plagued with feelings of anger and resentment that have led to an increase in violence in our society. Additionally, fathers are kept from seeing their children if they cannot afford to pay the exorbitant amounts of child support ordered by our courts. Some fathers are incarcerated for not being able to comply fully with court orders for child support. What good does it do to incarcerate a father who cannot afford to pay his child support obligation? If you incarcerate the father, he will lose his job, thereby making it impossible for him to pay his child support obligation in the future. Added to that, society now has to pay to house that father in jail and give the mother welfare benefits to help support their children. Even more importantly, the children of these incarcerated fathers are precluded from an ongoing, meaningful, loving relationship with them. Some of these father/child relationships are never mended as the mothers brainwash their innocent minds by telling them that their fathers refused to support them so the court had to put them in jail. The effect of this kind of emotional abuse on children is long-lasting.

My firm strictly represents men who are experiencing these types of situations. Men's rights law firms are opening throughout the country. Approximately 95% of our clients are men. About 80% of our cases consist of a mother who refuses to allow the father to see their children for a whole host of absurd reasons. Once separated, these fathers who were previously known as loving and caring men while married are suddenly labeled as wife beaters, drug addicts, alcoholics, molesters or simply "crazy." Once the allegations are made, the men have the burden of disproving the allegations. Men are considered guilty from the outset of the case and must prove their innocence. While attempting to prove their innocence, men are prohibited from seeing their children in an effort to "protect" the children, or their visitation may be supervised. After months or years of litigation to prove that the allegations were false, the men are finally reunited with their children who are now angry, confused and bitter because of the separation. Mothers fight to keep fathers from seeing their children mostly for monetary reasons. The less time the father sees the children the more child support he is forced to pay. It is a business. Most of our cases would be easily settled if not for the greed of the mothers. These children become pawns in a sick game by the mother to "get even" with her ex-husband or to gain a monetary advantage.

It's not uncommon for mothers who are awarded exorbitant child support amounts by the court to send the children to spend time with their father so that they can live the lifestyle they believe they "deserve" or to spend more time with their "current" boyfriend. They wait until after the court order is issued because child support is based on the amount of overnights that the parents spend with the children. If the father has a significant number of overnights or a 50-50 timesharing plan and both parents earn equal salaries, there would be no exchange of child support. Once the divorce action is final, there is no reason not to allow the father to see the children as much as he wants.

There are many fathers, who will agree to pay a larger child support amount in order to spend more time with the children. In fact, most mothers will give the fathers a 50-50 timesharing schedule if they agree to a larger child support amount. For most men, it is not about the money but about their continued relationship with their children.

Most of our clients are really good fathers who are simply trying to continue to play an active role in their children's lives but they are prevented from doing so by the mothers. There are circumstances where other emotions are involved. For example, the wife may be angry over the pending divorce because the father has left her for another woman. Even in these situations, it is important to put the child's needs before the needs or desires of either parent. Children suffer because of the parents' inability to properly parent, which means putting the children's needs before their own.

There is a whole host of other reasons mothers fight fathers over timesharing of the children. Sometimes they have not emotionally processed the divorce yet. In many cases, they are shocked by the filing and service of the divorce papers and they use the children as a way to "get even" with their spouse. In a number of these scenarios, the mother will go to the courthouse to file a frivolous domestic violence petition just to keep the father away from the children even when no evidence exists to support the allegations. The courts enter domestic violence injunctions on the slimmest of allegations. The courts conclude that there is a divorce pending so the parties should be kept apart. Judges are afraid that if they do not give the woman the injunction and remove the man from the home they might be chastised if there is an act of violence in the future. There have been instances where the court did not enter the injunction and the woman was physically injured or killed and the question was asked, "Why didn't you issue an injunction?" In many cases, the allegations and woman's testimony only amounts to a "fear" of domestic violence but there is no actual physical abuse. In accordance with the statute, there must be fear of violence and some overt act on the part of the aggressor. The overt act that is required is usually not present. In most cases, the woman will arrive in court, testify that she is in fear, display a few tears and/or appear very emotional. Judges err on the side of caution and are reluctant not to issue the injunction.

If a temporary domestic violence injunction is issued, the father is prohibited from being within 500 feet of the marital home, he has his constitutional right to bear arms temporarily or permanently suspended, and the mother is awarded one hundred percent of the timesharing with the children. After the father is ordered to have no contact with the children, the timesharing issue is referred to the judge who is going to handle the divorce. The vast majority of domestic violence cases are filed by women. There are women's shelters set up to house and protect women, as well as the children, if they should need housing, counseling and/or other protective measures. They can go to these shelters with the children; the fathers are precluded from going there or seeing their children because of the injunction. These injunctions can stay in place for a set period of time or indefinitely. Once a domestic violence injunction is ordered, it will affect the divorce case in regard to the father's timesharing with the children. Domestic violence is one of the factors the court can use to determine the best interests of the children when forming a timesharing and parenting plan.

Now the father has yet another hurdle to jump to become an active participant in his children's lives. With an injunction entered, usually because of an argument that occurred between the husband and wife, the court only sees the words "domestic violence injunction" and believes that there was some type of ongoing physical violence perpetrated by the father upon the mother. Because of the way that our court system works, there is little time for an unprepared attorney to delve into the allegations and facts surrounding the underlying domestic violence case. The judge views this mother as being beaten repeatedly by the father and does not realize it was just a marital disagreement. Therefore, fathers are at a disadvantage going into court as they try to get beyond the mindset that the judge has regarding the alleged domestic violence. Many judges still believe that mothers are better caregivers for children, even though psychological studies and the law states otherwise. Therefore, the way an attorney will deal with this situation depends on knowing the judge assigned to the case, knowing what views the judge has on parenting and knowing the ability of his client to parent his child.

If the judge assigned to a case has "old fashioned" views on gender preferences regarding custody decisions, we inform our client that it would be in his best interest to hire a parenting evaluator, or coordinator. The evaluator is usually a psychologist who will perform a full investigation including talking to both of the parents, the children, pediatrician, school, teachers, relatives, police and anyone else that either parent feels should be interviewed. If the children are involved in any kind of sports, the evaluator will contact the coaches and anyone else who has interaction with the children at these events. The best witnesses are independent third parties who do not have a stake in the proceeding. Teachers and coaches make excellent witnesses as they have firsthand knowledge of the parent's interaction with the children and participation in either the activity or school itself. Teachers know which parent is involved in helping the children with their homework, who shows up for parent-teacher conferences and who has a hands-on role in the children's education. Additionally, the children's pediatrician is a good source of information as he or she knows which parent is calling when the children are sick, and who is bringing the children into the office for wellness checks or emergency visits, shots and for annual exams. Sometimes it is one parent regularly involved in medical care, sometimes it is both, other times the parents bring the children in when it is that particular parent's time with the children.

The third party witnesses provide information to the evaluator that is eventually compiled into a formal report. The report is filed with the court. Included in the report is a recommendation as to what is in the best interest of the children and what the court should order as a timesharing schedule and parenting plan. This is based on the evaluator's knowledge, investigation, experience and education. More importantly, the evaluator can be subpoenaed to appear at a hearing to testify, especially in cases where the mother has made false allegations against the father. The expert has investigated those allegations and can opine as to the validity of them. It is difficult to defend against allegations of alcohol or drug abuse, sexual misconduct against the children or inappropriate parenting techniques without an expert. It becomes a "he said" and "she said" scenario with judges erring on the side of caution with a mindset of protecting the children. Most of these types of allegations are made to keep the father away from the children, or and made out of anger or fear, or an attempt "to get even" with the father. Frequently, a father can prevail and overcome these claims with an expert assigned to the case. In some cases, the mother will amend her pleadings after an evaluator is assigned or requested, because of the fear that she will be "found out" and the allegations will be revealed as frivolous. Other times, the allegations are that the father was not hands-on with the rearing of the children when, in fact, he was very active in the lives of his children. The evaluator will then be able to opine that the father did attend pediatrician appointments and teacher conferences, was active in the children's education, did homework with the children, attended sporting events and coached teams, all of which contradicts the mother's allegations.

Some mothers make the allegations in an attempt to get the upper hand in a divorce. In a number of our cases, it is the father who is the better parent. Most fathers are willing to facilitate contact with the mother and encourage her participation with the children going forward. Many times the judges are trying to place the children with the parent they feel will be least acrimonious. Most judges are astute at seeing through mothers who are trying to alienate the father from the children. They sometimes will grant custody of the children to the father because they believe that the father will follow the court's order by providing the mother contact with the children.

Judges are slowly changing their archaic mindset and realizing that fathers care more about the best interest of the children and are not looking for money from the mother. The father is more willing to work with the mother regarding schedules if there are changes in circumstances. Maybe the mother cannot get the children as ordered or the father has to work late. This commitment to the family continues after the divorce is final and alleviates the need for post-dissolution court intervention. Judges seek to do what is in the best interest of the children and they find that there is a decrease in litigation when fathers are given equal or extensive timesharing with the children. This is good for judicial economy as the court can direct its attention to other more important matters. The fact is that most fathers are hands-on and want to be a part of their children's upbringing. As a law firm, we are focused on father's rights and we have an excellent reputation in the community. Over the years, the judges in the surrounding counties have become aware that once our firm signs on to represent a father that we aggressively fight to secure him whatever rights he is entitled to.

DOMESTIC VIOLENCE ISSUES

Domestic violence is on the rise in Florida. A combination of stress from the economy, the collapse of the housing market and changes in the law has made it easier for a person to obtain a civil injunction against domestic violence. It is important for people to know what constitutes domestic violence, its definition and its impact on their rights to see their children during and after the divorce. In some cases, the domestic violence is apparent on its face because there are pictures of bruises or other injuries, witness statements, admissions made to police officers, medical reports detailing the injuries, and information about how they were inflicted. Violence that causes these types of injuries is what the law was originally enacted to protect against. Due to the rise of domestic violence reported to police or the courts, the legislature realized that there was a need to protect women against abusive spouses. It was not just a "family" problem. Many women are smaller in stature when compared to men and arguments sometimes escalate, becoming physical in nature. In years past, when there was a report of domestic violence, the police would be called to "calm" the situation down. Police reports were taken but most of the time the police would ask the male spouse to leave the residence to cool off for the night before being allowed to come back home the next day. The couple worked out their differences the best that they could and as they saw fit for the whole family.

Going back to the 40's, 50's and into the 60's, women were more dependent on their husbands for financial support. They did not work outside the home; therefore, they had no way to support themselves and their children. Even without physical violence, there may have been many verbal arguments but wives were reluctant to do anything about it because they had no other place to go and they wanted to keep the family intact. They needed a roof over their head and food on the table for their children. Once women moved into the work force and were able to support themselves, the domestic violence laws passed were not only strengthened but the level of proof for an injunction degraded considerably. Initially there needed to be some actual physical altercation and/or injury. The statute regarding domestic violence in Florida now allows for the issuance of an injunction if the woman testifies that she is in fear of domestic violence. Somebody could go into court and say, "We had this argument and I am afraid that he is going to hurt me." However, according to the statute there has to be some type of overt act, like a hand being raised to smack, that causes the fear. In most cases, what we see is a couple having marital problems, an argument ensuing and escalating and a threat to leave or take the children being made. Without the overt act needed by statute, judges are reluctant not to issue the domestic violence injunction. They are afraid of the ramifications of sending the couple back home together and the argument escalating into violence that possibly causes serious bodily injury or death.

Knowing that the courts are reluctant to dismiss a domestic violence case without putting protections in place to keep the couple apart, there are attorneys who advise women to file for an injunction in an attempt to get the upper hand in a soon-to-be-filed divorce. Included in the domestic violence final judgment are provisions for exclusive use and possession of the home, timesharing, a parenting plan, child support and alimony. The temporary injunction is entered solely based on the allegations contained in the petition. As long as the magic word "fear" is in the petition, a temporary injunction is issued without a hearing or notice to the husband. Subsequently, the husband is served, usually at his home by the sheriff, and is escorted from the home and told that he cannot return until further order of the court. He cannot see his children during the time between the date he is served and the final hearing, which is typically scheduled for two weeks from the time of service. If the husband does not have any friends, family or resources, he could be left homeless until the hearing.

After the hearing, the wife usually remains in the marital home and the husband is not allowed within 500 feet of the home. The wife will get 100% timesharing with the children, sole parental responsibility, and child support and alimony that are calculated using guesstimates, as there is not sufficient time to prepare accurate financial affidavits. The process amounts to a fifteen-minute hearing, if it lasts that long, and settles many of the divorce issues. Most attorneys do not realize that they are entitled to discovery, such as depositions and requests for discovery, as well as the calling of witnesses at the hearing. We find it important to take the wife's deposition, contact the police officer who took the report and seek any and all witnesses to the domestic violence. We usually serve subpoenas to police officers, neighbors, family members and even children, if they were witnesses to the alleged altercation. Without this intensive pre-trial discovery and full and fair hearing, the client will be left behind the eight ball and in a defensive posture during the divorce proceedings. The presumption that is tied to domestic violence as being detrimental to children is hard to overcome.

As part of our basic constitutional rights, the husband is entitled to a full and fair hearing. Unfortunately, there are many men who do not take a domestic violence case seriously. They assume that they will show up in court, explain that they just had a misunderstanding and it will just go away; therefore, they attend the hearing unprepared and without counsel. The hearing begins and ends before the husband has a chance to breathe much less present any evidence. Often, it only requires a tear or two from the wife to convince the judge to find that she is in fear and to issue the injunction, usually before all testimony and evidence is presented. With proper representation, it is possible for the husband to avoid trial altogether through discovery. If that fails, it is possible to agree to a no contact order in the divorce case and dismissal of the domestic violence case altogether. This gives the wife the protection that she needs because the husband is not allowed to go to the marital home but there is no finding in a judgment that domestic violence occurred. In this scenario the husband will have to deal with that issue in the upcoming divorce case.

In some instances, a civil domestic violence case will be accompanied by a criminal proceeding for the same set of facts. The husband is usually arrested at the scene and the wife is told to obtain a civil injunction as well. This adds an additional dimension to the handling of the civil case as both cases are working their way through the legal system simultaneously. As far as the civil case is concerned, the attorney has to be extremely careful not to implicate the client by having him testify, as this could be detrimental to him in the criminal case. Most of the time, it is advisable to have the client refuse to incriminate himself, by asserting his Fifth Amendment protections against self-incrimination. Unfortunately, the downside is that the injunction will probably be issued based solely on the testimony of the wife. The upside is that the injunction will state that the husband did not defend because his constitutional right was invoked. Additionally, the client can agree to the injunction without a hearing; therefore, there would be no findings of fact in the final judgment. The husband is faced with a dilemma. He cannot testify because anything he says can and will be used against him in the criminal case. These ramifications can be devastating. It is usually assumed that he did not testify because he did not want to incriminate himself in the criminal case. If the attorney is able to get the criminal domestic violence case dismissed, there is the possibility that the civil case can be reopened and possibly have the civil injunction set aside at a later date.

Sometimes mothers will file a request for a domestic violence injunction on behalf of the children or if the children were witnesses to the alleged violence, they allege that the court needs to protect the children through injunctive relief. The father will have no contact with either the wife or children while the injunction is in place. It could be several months before the husband has the opportunity to go before the judge handling the divorce to be able to see his children. In these instances, the timesharing is usually supervised, or therapeutically supervised. Modifying these temporary orders is difficult and gives the wife leverage regarding other issues in the divorce case such as alimony and equitable distribution.

Domestic violence becomes a huge hurdle to negotiate when you attempt mediation, especially if the case goes to trial. The mothers usually use it as leverage to try to settle the case in a way that is most beneficial to them. If the attorney does not strategically plan the domestic violence case and divorce case simultaneously, the father usually receives less timesharing with the children, or supervised timesharing, which means they pay more child support. Sometimes the mothers use the domestic violence judgment as leverage to obtain more of the assets, or to receive more alimony, or alimony for a longer duration of time. Once the mother has everything she wants, she will often agree to dismiss the domestic violence case.

In many cases, the wives are the initial instigators of the violence. We find that in these cases, the wife will start the altercation by pointing a finger, prodding or poking the husband, and then when the husband attempts to defend himself, even simply arguing back, pointing back or pushing back, the wife contacts the police. Sometimes the wife will self-inflict various wounds before the police arrive on the scene. She will bang her arms to cause bruising, smack herself and bang her head on the wall to cause fresh bruises. Once the police arrive, the husband is taken to jail for domestic violence. The police take pictures of the bruises that were self-inflicted and later these pictures, along with the police testimony and/or reports, are used against the husband at the trial in the civil and criminal domestic violence cases. It is very difficult to defend these cases because there are rarely any independent witnesses. It is a "he said" and "she said" type of scenario.

At our firm, we like to depose the wife before we go into any court proceeding. During those depositions, the wife will realize she is under oath and under penalty of perjury must tell the truth. It is then that her testimony will be different from the allegations that she swore were correct in the petition for domestic violence or police report. Sometimes we are able to get the wife to agree to dismiss the domestic violence case to avoid having the state attorney go forward with a criminal perjury action against her. Perjury, or lying under oath, is a criminal offense. She may have told other people, she may have told friends or family members before she applied for an injunction that she was planning to file one just to get the husband out of the house. Sometimes she will tell other people that she intends to lie to get the injunction. Subpoenas sent to these witnesses or the taking of their deposition prior to the trial is sometimes enough to convince the wife to dismiss the case.

At the domestic violence hearing, the attorney for the wife will usually ask if she will be able to live in the same home with the husband while the divorce is pending. When the wife answers that it would be awkward, the conversation turns to how they can remove the husband from the marital home. If the wife states that the husband will not go peacefully by agreeing to leave, then it may be suggested that an injunction be sought. This is usually followed by an argument at the house that night over who should leave the home while the upcoming divorce is pending. Usually the husband has no place to go so he stands his ground in order to keep a roof over his head and stay close to his children. The argument escalates, the police are called and the scenario plays out. The accusations in these cases usually stem from an argument that the couple had about the usual marital problems such as sex, money or the children. If the couple had been able to communicate better, they probably would not be seeking a divorce. Other times there is already a third party involved, a new boyfriend or girlfriend, and when jealously is added to an already tense situation, emotions run high.

The wife is usually awarded exclusive use and possession of the marital home, and sole custody of the children, and a trial is scheduled within 14 days. The wife is well on her way to getting everything she wanted in the divorce proceedings without ever having the case heard. At the final hearing, child support is calculated and the husband is not afforded any timesharing with the children, as that issue is reserved for the judge who is handling the divorce. Also, there are cases where temporary alimony is ordered. The wife is now in a superior position in the divorce case and the husband has to grovel to see his children. Many of these fathers were hands-on caregivers of the children. Some of the mothers were either employed outside the home and the breadwinners for the family, may already have a boyfriend in the background, or could care less about the children. It becomes about dollars and how many dollars she can get from the husband. The children are used as pawns in an effort to acquire a superior financial position.

Immediately upon being served with a temporary injunction, it benefits the husband greatly to seek legal representation. Without proper representation, he will be at a terrible disadvantage. The attorney should have experience in the domestic violence court for that particular county. It is heartbreaking to have a client come into our office with a final judgment of injunction after a trial where he had hired a real estate attorney to represent him, rather than an experienced family attorney. An attorney who does not know the ins and outs of domestic violence law, or one whp takes the issuance of an injunction as "no big deal," does a great disservice to his client. These lawyers do not realize they are entitled to discovery, including depositions, requests for production of records, police reports, witnesses testimony and a full and fair hearing, or simply the request for a continuance so that the client can have a fair trial. It is not possible for an attorney to properly prepare for a trial in the time afforded after service of the temporary injunction. Most of the time, the temporary injunction is served a day, or a few days, before the scheduled trial.

Many of these husbands show up in court alone and without representation. The thought process is "We just had another disagreement and I was unjustly put out of my home and, once I tell my story to the judge, he will find out that she pushed me first and the case will be dismissed." With this mindset, the husband is doomed for failure. The domestic violence court is set up to protect women. There are people situated in the courtroom who will meet with the wife upon her arrival. They work for battered women shelters or similar organizations. They will instruct the wife to go forward even if they know that she was not a victim of violence. Some wives come to their senses before the hearing and want to dismiss the case because they realize that it was just another disagreement that got out of hand emotionally. However, once counseled by the representatives of the shelter, most women are swayed to go forward to obtain the injunction. Some women are counseled on their testimony and counseled on how to act in front of the judge. Sometimes these representatives will escort the wife to the bench and stand by her side during the trial. When the husband arrives, he is segregated from the wife and placed on the opposite end of the courtroom. Any contact with the wife will be a violation of the injunction and subject the husband to incarceration.

The hearings are over in a matter of minutes. The husband is usually left with his jaw hanging in disbelief. Sometimes there are thirty or more cases to be heard in a couple of hours, so time is the controlling factor rather than justice. Cases usually last five to ten minutes, and with the pounding of the gavel, the husband has lost everything he holds dear to him - - his children. Many times the husband is not given the chance to participate. The wife puts on such a convincing show through her testimony that the court has already decided to issue the injunction without any defense from the husband. When these men enter our doors, the conversation typically goes something like this, "I don't know what happened. I walked in, was called up to the bench and then it was over. I was handed these papers. What do I have to do now to see my children and get back into my home? My wife told a bunch of lies to the judge and he believed her."

Once entered, final judgments are very difficult to get dissolved. A motion can be filed and a hearing set, but all the wife has to do is show up in court and state that "she is still in fear" of domestic violence and the final judgment will stand. The injunction will remain in place indefinitely. When the injunction is entered for a short period of time, say a year, the wife will file a motion to continue the injunction just prior to its expiration claiming she is still in fear. A hearing will be set, but in most cases the injunction will be extended for an additional period of time or indefinitely. Most injunctions are entered and remain in effect until further order of the court, which means indefinitely.

I cannot overemphasize the importance of retaining competent counsel immediately after being served with the temporary injunction. It is crucial in the scheme of things to protect your basic constitutional right to due process by vigorously litigating these cases so that you obtain a full and fair hearing.

(This content should be used for informational purposes only. It does not create an attorney-client relationship with any reader and should not be construed as legal advice. If you need legal advice, please contact an attorney in your community who can assess the specifics of your situation.)

Julie Bauknight
Law Firm of Julie Bauknight
Victoria, Texas

Julie is the voice of reason with clients going through divorce. She is firm and fair, but knows how to pull off the gloves to make sure her clients get a fair division of marital property, equitable child support and workable plans for visitation and child custody. As a mother of four children, her number one priority throughout the process is the best interest of the children.

ARE TEMPORARY ORDERS – TEMPORARY?

One of the first questions people want to know the answer to is how long the process of getting a divorce will take. In Texas, you are required to wait at least 60 days before a divorce is finalized. In reality, unless you come into an attorney's office together as husband and wife and are agreeable to the divorce, and have a simple divorce with few assets, it's almost impossible to have it done within 60 days. Realistically, if it's not a really antagonistic situation, probably six months to a year would be the average length of time.

If I encounter a potential client who is unsure about whether he or she really wants a divorce, and requires a broader understanding of the process and the possible result, I will explain the process, and emphasize that once a divorce is filed, it's not finalized right away. Different states have different waiting periods; but, as I stated, Texas has a 60-day waiting period, and that's the earliest the divorce could be finalized.

If a married couple starts the process and they go to counseling to try to save their marriage, the divorce action can be left pending until they're ready to move forward. I always let them know that it is possible to dismiss the action once it's been filed. It just depends on the couple. Sometimes it's helpful for them to have the divorce proceedings started and have temporary orders put in place. That gives them some ground rules as they work through counseling to try to fix their marriage. The other thing I tell them is that one of my jobs as an attorney is to discern whether reconciliation is an option.

It's amazing sometimes how much hope that gives people. They want to know there's an option to back out if there's still hope for the marriage. You can leave a divorce pending for quite some time without really taking any action. That way you don't have to start the process all over again if reconciliation doesn't work out.

If the husband or wife is certain they want a divorce, then I focus more on the steps and procedures. We talk about filing for a divorce and getting the temporary orders in place so that this person is protected. The purpose of temporary orders is to keep the status quo. Running their business, managing their finances, and paying their bills, will all be maintained with a temporary order. That's also the point in time to look at allegations of violence in the home, and to determine whether they need some further level of protection, such as getting the other spouse out of the house or limiting access to them or to the children. This would depend on actions that took place prior to the filing of the divorce.

A frequently-asked question is, "How long do those temporary orders continue during the process of obtaining a divorce?" Temporary orders don't have a time limit on them. The wording of the order itself says, "These remain the order of the court until they are changed by agreement or the court creates further orders."

If the situation changes, you can file a modification of temporary orders. I've had situations where the mom has custody of the children, and six months down the road under the temporary orders, one of the children turns 13 or 14 years old and says, "I want to go and live with Dad," and both parents agree to the change. You can modify the temporary orders to adjust the child support or adjust whatever bills are getting paid, because you now have a split-custody situation. If the orders are not changed, they stay in place until you reach an agreement on your final order or when you go to court, have a hearing, and get the final orders for your case.

In our society, it's usually the woman who is more dependent on the husband's salary. It's comforting for the wife to know that bills are going to be paid by having these temporary orders. I have to tell the spouse who is making more money that it's going to be a little painful during this process and during the temporary orders, because typically the other party moves to an apartment, or moves in with another family.

Consequently, in addition to maintaining the marital home, he or she will have the expense of an apartment rental.

A common problem we face in divorce cases is that people get advice from their family and friends. People will say, "Well, you know, my friend has three kids and when they got divorced, they had shared custody, and the dad was still paying child support," etc., etc. They think, "Well, because I have three kids and we want to do this, it should work the same way." The fact is, they don't know all the facts of the other case intimately.

When getting advice from other people, one must realize that no two cases are alike, and based on the situation, the result may not be the same.

Another problem we often face is that people think that every judge and every court will treat their situation in the same way, but that's not the case. We have the law, but there's also room for discretion by the court. There are many variables that can affect the judge's ruling. It may be something as simple as the dad getting on the stand and displaying a horrible attitude, being rude to the attorneys, and being rude to the judge. The judge has the discretion and authority, because he or she is observing character and therefore, the credibility of that character, to look at the dad and think, "I don't find what he's telling me to be credible," even though it might be. Because that party gave such a bad impression to the court the court might rule more favorably towards the mom. Therefore, when friends tell you what you can expect to happen in your case, you need to take their advice with a pinch of salt.

ISSUES THAT SURROUND CHILD CUSTODY

The first thing parents want to know is who will have custody of the children, and how custody will be split. Firstly, you look at who has been doing the daily caretaking of the children. We start with the status quo, but it's inevitable that things will change. For instance, if you have a stay-at-home mom who's done everything for the kids and dad's been at work, that doesn't mean that Dad's a bad parent. It's just that the normality has been mom as the caretaker. Typically, it would stay that way, but no matter what, dad has to have visitation with his children. Consequently, during his time with the children, he will have to learn how to be the caretaker and do everything that mom would have done.

That's a general starting point. There could be a situation where the parents are doing shift work and they work on opposite shifts. In reality, those parents are equal caregivers of the child, and there could be a battle over which parent wants to be the primary parent. If both parents are working, it is legitimate for the court to look at the jobs of the respective parents. One parent may have a job with long hours, where the children are often in the care of someone else, and the other parent may have a more flexible work schedule or better hours, so that there's still time spent with the children. In Texas, we now have the ability to make the parents completely equal and declare the county where the child resides as the primary residence of the child. In that way, if the parents have joint custody, (week on/week off, two weeks on/two weeks off) with the children, one person doesn't have more rights than the other.

Next, the courts are going to look at the home situation. Sometimes, the mom has been the primary caregiver of the children, but she's never worked outside the home. Now, due to the divorce situation, she's going to have to get a job. She's going to have to move in with family members or friends in the interim just to get back on her feet. If the father is awarded the home where the children live, the court may decide that it's less disruptive to the children to remain in the home that they know, rather than with their mom who has mostly taken care of them.

The court can also look at the environment where the children will live. If mom has to double up with another family, then the court's going to want to know what space this child will have for him or herself. Will they be forced to share a room with other relatives/cousins/older people? All these aspects can be considered, and are often looked upon as less-than-ideal situations for a child.

The courts will try to ensure that the children remain in the same school district. If the child has to transition to an unfamiliar school, the courts can consider that factor. The courts have a major catch-all criterion which is "the best interest of the child." It provides a great deal of discretion in deciding what really is best for the child.

Couples getting a divorce always want to know at what age a child's preference will be taken into consideration with respect to where he or she might live. Under Texas law, there is a provision for children under the age of three. It's not a mandatory provision, but it is something that can be brought up. Let's say you have a very young child whose dad has never really taken care of him, and mom has never gone out of town and left the child overnight with the dad. Such a young child requires a greater level of care from a parent, and this dad, being inexperienced, is not prepared for that. You can ask for a special provision that until that child reaches the age of three, there won't be any overnights with the other parent, just day visits. They can be shorter, more frequent visits, rather than long visits that include overnight. This also gives dad a transition time to acquire the skills required to care for a young child.

The other age of significance in Texas is 12. At that age the court can consider the child's wishes regarding who they would like to have as their primary parent, or who they would like to live with. Some changes are coming in Texas, but right now the court says that until a child is 12 years old, when it is time for the other parent to have visitation, your job as the primary parent is to put that child in the car and make him go, even if he is refusing to go, and is kicking and screaming.

Once the child turns 12, then your job shifts to just having the child available for the visitation. If Dad's coming to pick the child up at 6 p.m., then you need to be home with the child, and have him available and ready to go. Then if the child refuses to go, at least your duty is fulfilled, and you can't be held in contempt of court.

At age 14, the child's choice is given more weight by the court, and it's not just that they may consider it. The exception may be a 14-year-old child who has the maturity level of a 10-year-old. That type of situation gives you some room to argue that this child does not know what's in his own best interest and is picking the other parent for inappropriate reasons, e.g., the other parent's house doesn't have any rules or curfews, or maybe Dad's been allowing the child to smoke, or something of that nature.

The reality is that with an older child, aged 14, 15, or 16, if you tell that child, "I'm sorry. I know you want to live with your dad, but I'm making you live with your mom," then anybody who knows teenagers, knows that this will be a miserable situation for everyone involved, because that child is going to rebel. You also run the risk of having a child who threatens, "Fine. Put me in Dad's house and I'll run away." Now you're looking at the safety of the child. When he's 16 years old, there's really not much the court or the parent can do to make him comply.

INSIGHTS INTO CHILD VISITATION

Child visitation is a huge issue to deal with in a divorce. In Texas, we have the Standard Possession Order. It sets the structure known as first, third, and fifth weekends. Basically, the non-custodial parent has the child on the first, third, and fifth weekends of every month, and then there's a structure for holidays. Typically, if one parent has the child for Thanksgiving, then the other parent is going to have him for Christmas that year. The Christmas holiday is divided in half, and it starts on whatever day the school gets out for the Christmas holidays. That period of possession for a parent ends at noon on the 28th. Then the other parent would have from noon on the 28th until six o'clock on the Sunday before school resumes. Spring break alternates between parents.

Another consideration is other holidays that are important to the family. You can make provisions for them, but otherwise, they're not assigned. In regard to the child's birthday, if you are not otherwise entitled to have the child on the day of that child's birthday, then you may have the child from 6 to 8 p.m. on the birthday. You can also elect to have the other minor siblings be part of that window of visitation on that child's birthday. Then, of course, Mother's Day weekend always goes to Mom, and Father's Day weekend always goes to Dad. In the summer time, the non-custodial parent gets a 30-day block of time, and the schedule kind of "flip-flops" because during that 30-day block, the other parent can choose a weekend to have the child, so they don't go an entire 30 days without seeing them. These rules all apply to parents who live fewer than 100 miles apart.

If you live more than 100 miles apart, the holidays stay the same. You can still continue the first, third, and fifth weekends. If that's not feasible, then you can do the alternative schedule, which is one weekend per month, but you get to choose whichever weekend in that month that you want. This scenario also changes spring break, in that the non-custodial parent has spring break every single year, and then the summer possession goes from 30 days to 42 days. The other parent then gets two weekends during that 42-day period block. One thing that I like to point out to people is that the details of a possession order are covered over pages and pages of documentation. It gives detailed definitions and says things like, "Whatever belonging the child takes for his visitation should be brought home with the child," and "If you can't pick the child up or drop them off, you're entitled to designate a competent adult to drive for you."

At the very beginning of the order, there is a paragraph entitled, "Mutual Agreement," that says that the parents of this child may have possession and access to the child at any time it is mutually agreed to in advance by both parties. The whole intent of that paragraph is to tell these people, "You two are the parents of these kids. You know what's best for them. You should be able to figure out what works and what doesn't. And here's your complete power to do that. In the event you can't reach an agreement, here are your eight pages of detailed instructions on how to manage your child."

INSIGHTS INTO CHILD SUPPORT

Child support will be paid by the parent who is not the primary parent. This is another area where people can agree to do what they want to do, but there are state guidelines for determining the amount of child support to be paid, and it's based on the net income of the person.

Child support comes into effect and stays in effect until the child turns 18 years of age or graduates from high school, whichever is later. If you have a child who turns 18 in April and graduates in June, your child support will be payable through the month of June.

The rule in Texas is that if nobody has done anything with regard to child support, or reviewed it for the last three years, then it's automatically eligible for review to determine what changes need to be made. The same thing happens with health insurance. The courts are very intent on making sure that there is health insurance coverage for the children in one form or another. If dad is paying child support, and he has no health insurance through his job but mom's job has health insurance, then you just have Dad reimburse Mom the premium amount. If Dad has the health insurance and he's paying the child support, then he just continues to keep the kids covered.

Another issue that occurs is a parent wanting to increase visitation time just to decrease child support. I've seen many people who are absolutely gung-ho on split custody. They want to do a week on/week off, and it has absolutely nothing to do with the time that they get with their child. It has to do with the premise that if we have him the same number of days, neither of us should pay child support. There are some ways around that though, because you can do an offset. You can say,

"Okay, well, if dad were paying child support for this child to mom, he would pay $500 a month based on his wages. If Mom were paying child support to Dad for this same child based on her wages, she'd be paying $300 a month. The difference is $200, so Dad; you need to pay $200 a month in child support." You can offset it that way to make it a little bit more equal, especially if there's a huge disparity in income.

INSIGHTS INTO POST-DIVORCE MODIFICATIONS

Another obvious point is that life happens, circumstances change, and often modifications must be made to the divorce decree. You can't go back and modify your property division, but child support and visitation can be changed. Children grow up and their needs change, and any number of things can happen in their lives or the parent's lives, including remarriage, relocation, and/or new employment. Special needs may develop for the child, or, as the child gets older, he or she may say, "I'd really rather go and live in the other parent's house now."

The law allows you to modify visitation based on possession and access to the child, or modify based on support, or do a combination if both things need to be addressed, as they often do. Most of the time, modification is driven by the child support amount. If a person has been paying a low amount, but has been in a new job for several years now, and is making more money, the other party is likely to file for a modification in child-support payments.

Health insurance benefits could also trigger a modification. If you had a job with coverage and you've lost that job, or you've changed to a new job that doesn't provide health insurance, then you need to get this child covered, so you can go in and get a modification. As far as possession and access go, any number of factors could require a change in the plan.

When couples first get divorced, they usually have a very basic visitation plan. At some point, one parent may want to spend more time with the kids, but they may be met on the other side with "No, sorry.

144

This is your schedule. This is all you get." That parent may want to go back in and ask for more time. Changing from one parent's house to the other's isn't the only reason for modification. It can just be just a parent saying, "I want to spend more time with my child."

There are also situations where parents take a bad path and are involved in drugs, or have developed an addiction, and they're not caring for the child when they have visitation or maybe they've gone months or a year without seeing the child. Now suddenly, they've popped back in the picture, and they want to start right where they left off and pick this child up for a weekend. The other parent is saying, "Are you kidding? You haven't seen this child in a year. This child doesn't know you." So the primary parent goes back to court to modify, to have visitation reduced. The whole process can be started all over again if you have an addiction situation, for example. You could go back to a point where that parent's access to the child is supervised, and they have to do a step-by-step plan where little by little, they increase the time, and build back up to a standard possession order.

When people are seeking an arrangement like that, I tell them that no matter what happens, the court system always keeps its eye on the goal of standard possession, the minimum time that a parent should have with his or her child.

Sometimes, people want the other parent's visitation taken away forever. That's something we can't do, unless it's a really horrible situation where we need to consider terminating the rights of the parent completely. In general, despite mistakes in life or bad choices, we must keep the goal of maintaining that parent-child relationship.

Relocation is an issue that frequently requires modification of the order. About three years ago, it became routine for Texas to place a geographical restriction on an order. Before that, you had to prove why you wanted a restriction on a parent. Now, if you ask for it, the court will give it to you. It became an issue because there actually are people who will move for no other purpose than to make visitation difficult, and to get the children away so that the other parent can't be part of the children's lives, just out of spite. The purpose of the restriction is to prevent people from doing that.

By placing a geographical restriction, you're erecting a stopping block so that now, if this parent wants to move, they have the extra burden of going back to the court and telling the court their reason for wanting to move. If the relocation is because of a job, they can come in to the court and say, "I was making $10 an hour here at this job, and then was offered a job 300 miles away, at $20 an hour. The school systems there are great, and I have some family support." If they can give a legitimate reason for moving, the chances are the court is going to allow them to move. They just don't want to endorse a situation where you have no reason to move other than to punish the other parent.

I've had some cases where the restriction encompasses just the State of Texas, wherein you can move anywhere within the state, but if you want to cross the state borders, you're going to have to get permission. Depending on their jobs, abilities, and finances, some people have more flexibility to overcome distances than others. Some states, like Louisiana, are very restrictive. They call it their Home State Rule. Even if the other parent moves away, it's almost impossible for you to move from the original town with the children. Most of the geographical restrictions in Texas specify that the restriction will be lifted at the point the other party moves away from the county.

The length of time required to get a modification can vary. It's going to depend on where you live and how clogged up the court system is in that area. The way the rules are in Texas are, if I were to file a modification based just on lifting a geographical restriction, I could file it and set it for a temporary order hearing within a couple of weeks. The problem is, in order to set anything for a final hearing; you have to give 45 days' notice. So if you wanted an absolute final ruling from the court, you'd have to file it, get that person served, and give them 45 days' notice before you could set a hearing. In that situation, I would recommend going the route of a temporary order, especially if it's a quick move. For instance, if you've received a new job offer and in three weeks you need to be there, ready to start your new job. Then you'd want a temporary order because more than likely, the ruling in the temporary order would be the same as the final order. If the other party was not fighting it and you filed that modification, you could end up with an agreed order, a final order that releases you right away.

MANIPULATING THE SYSTEM

Some women seemingly try to circumvent the formal divorce by getting a restraining order against their husband for alleged or actual violence. This happens quite frequently. Firstly, I can tell you I often file cases with a restraining order in the beginning, but there's a misconception on the part of the public as to what a restraining order is, at least in Texas. If you are a victim of family violence of any sort, then you probably will want to seek a protective order. You can also apply for a generic restraining order to keep the other party from being around you. That's what I do in my cases, and basically, it sets down some immediate rules for protection of property and assets.

A restraining order is not necessarily only designed for safety issues or because one person has done something very egregious. It's a way of saying, "We're going to shut everything down right now so that when you get these papers, you can't go clean out a bank account. You can't rack up a credit card. You can't remove somebody from the health insurance." You can basically freeze the status quo. The reasons that I do this are: one, it protects bank accounts; and two, it's a vehicle to get into court faster. A temporary restraining order is only good for a maximum of 14 days, so once you file it, you will obtain a temporary order setting a hearing within about 10 days from the day you filed.

A restraining order can be useful in a situation where parties aren't getting along at all, and the mom's not been working, and is absolutely panicked. She worries, "How are my bills going to be paid from now until we get into court? How am I going to buy food for my kids? He has all the money." A restraining order can put her mind at ease.

There can also be a temporary restraining order based on fear because of a past involving domestic violence. If there have been any domestic violence issues, we need to protect the person who has been subjected to that violence. The law in Texas requires me to attach an affidavit from the mom detailing an incident that occurred within the last 30 days which justifies this type of immediate action against the other person. That way, someone can't just get a temporary restraining order without facts to back it, just to make the other side look bad.

It can be advantageous, because now, this person gets served and in 10 days or less, he must be ready to go into court, with or without an attorney. So, if someone doesn't have the means to hire an attorney and he gets there for a temporary order hearing, that could be significantly advantageous to our side.

In this case, you're not seeking a protective order dealing with a situation where you have alleged horrible things about this person and tainted them in the court. A restraining order is more property-based. Even if the other party has an attorney, it's always better to be the attorney filing the restraining order, because you will have time to prepare for the hearing.

However, if the opposing attorney has filed a restraining order, and I've just been retained by a client, then I probably won't have sufficient time to prepare a case. Usually, unless there are extenuating circumstances, I can go to the hearing and inform the court, "I was only retained three days ago. I have not had sufficient time to prepare for this hearing and I need a continuation." This type of request is routinely granted.

The point that I want to make is that there are ways to protect you from harm from your spouse, be it physical or financial, but it is critical that you meet with a qualified attorney as quickly as possible. The longer you wait the more difficult it becomes to protect you and your children.

WHAT SHOULD ONE LOOK FOR IN HIRING AN ATTORNEY?

Several factors will influence your choice of an attorney. A lot has to do with personality. You are not going to be best friends with your attorney, but you need to be able to get along with his/her personality, and they must be able to get along with yours. You don't want to rub each other up the wrong way. There must be a level of communication that promotes trust between the two of you. I think it's a mistake in family law to retain a lawyer who's overly concerned with how many wins they have, or who guarantees the result they can get you in court. You're being misled if someone claims to be able to give guarantees.

The courts have so much discretion and there's so much variability to these types of situation that no two situations are going to end up with the same final order. I think it is okay to tell them, "In situations like yours, I have seen the courts award this, or they are more likely to award X, Y, Z than not." You can give them some general guidelines of what you've seen the court do, but just don't promise them a specific result.

With a divorce case, everything in it is personal. Clients have a lot of anxiety and concerns, and their whole life is changing. You want your attorney to recognize that you're a person going through this upheaval. It's not just dividing assets and moving on with your life. I really do enjoy talking to people and learning different things, and I enjoy conversing with a variety of people. Speaking for myself, I am genuinely interested in the outcome for these people. I do fully recognize this is not just a business transaction.

I hope that I never lose sight of the fact that I am dealing with real people and real lives. When their case is over, my involvement is finished, but whatever the outcome, that remains a part of their lives, and I think that's a very important thing to remember. There are times when my clients make decisions that I don't necessarily think are the best choices in their situation. But as long as I have done my job of laying out the pros and cons of their decision, and they understand the good and bad aspects of it, and they still choose to make that decision, that's the point in time that I have to step back and say, "I'm not the one who has to live with the consequences."

I had a man look at me one day, after I had explained to him that the property deal we had set up was probably losing him around $20,000. He looked me in the eye and said, "Ma'am, I know that. But you can't put a price on peace." I just thought that was a great moment, when the client reaffirmed that it was his life. It's my business, but it's their life. That's the perspective I always try to maintain.

(This content should be used for informational purposes only. It does not create an attorney-client relationship with any reader and should not be construed as legal advice. If you need legal advice, please contact an attorney in your community who can assess the specifics of your situation.)

Brian E. Arnold
Arnold & Wadsworth
Salt Lake City, UT

Brian is an Editor on the Utah Journal of Family Law where he works closely with judges and other attorneys in developing meaningful articles for Utah Attorneys that practice family law. Unlike most family law attorneys, Brian will take your case to trial if need be. If you are accused of cohabitation or think your former spouse is now cohabitation getting an attorney that can go to trial is essential.

FIRST, SECOND, AND THIRD DIVORCES

When someone is facing a divorce, emotions are running high, and he or she is experiencing a lot of anxiety. He or she knows that a divorce will have an impact on their whole life, including family dynamics, finances, and future expectations. I have found in Utah that the greatest concern is for their children. Each parent wants to know, "How am I going to get custody, or how am I going to prevent my spouse from getting custody of my children?" Other factors that people worry about in a divorce are alimony, property division, or any division of assets. They're about to have a judge tell them how drastically their lives are going to change.

One trend we are now experiencing is people coming in for their second or third divorces, trying to determine what property is premarital or not premarital. Utah is categorized as an "equitable division state," which does not always mean divided equally. There's a lot of gray area in the Utah law to argue for division of certain assets, alimony, or anything that deals with money. It's important to have the right kind of attorney who knows how to argue your case in front of a judge.

Many divorces are laden with emotion, to the extent that parties almost hate their spouses. When they meet with their attorney, they want you to dislike their spouse as much as they do. One thing I hear from clients is, "You know, if I can just get on that stand and tell the judge my side of the story, there's no way that the judge is going to disagree with me." The fact is that sometimes what you say isn't that relevant to what the judge is going to decide. A good attorney is going to calm you down and educate you to the fact that letting all your emotions out in the courtroom is not going to help you in any way.

Obviously, when someone is getting a divorce, things are very emotional, but one has to learn to look at it from a legal perspective, so one can get the outcome they want. He or she wants to look like the better, stronger adult in the relationship, in order to get custody or the alimony needed, or to avoid paying alimony. Credibility is always an issue in divorce. It's something that the judge constantly looks at, and that's why you need to keep your emotions in check from the beginning of a divorce.

THE DIFFERENCE BETWEEN A DIVORCE AND A LEGAL SEPARATION

What the law calls "legal separation" lasts for roughly a year. It's just like going through a divorce: you settle everything, including custody, asset division, and alimony, but the difference is that it doesn't last forever like a divorce does. Eventually, the court will ask you to come back to finalize your divorce or withdraw your petition. There is one circumstance where I see legal separation being very helpful to people, and that is one where you're working on your relationship, but you need to be apart, or if you're moving far away, but you're still working on your relationship. As you see, the key to legal separation is that you're working on your relationship, and if you are doing that, it can be a great tool to help you work on saving your marriage.

Most often we see a call for legal separation if one or both spouses have had affairs, and they're trying to work through the situation. Nevertheless, I always tell my clients, a legal separation often costs as much as a divorce, and it doesn't last as long. If you've definitely decided you're getting a divorce, you might as well get divorced. However, if you really are doing everything to save your marriage, legal separation is the best option.

One benefit of a legal separation is that you can stay on each other's health insurance. When you are divorced, your spouse can't stay on your health insurance. If there are health problems with one of the parties, this option may make sense, but it's important to remember that it only lasts for a short period of time.

Many people think that a legal separation is going to save them money from a legal perspective. Unless you reconcile, that's simply not true. Many times the couple re-litigates all the issues that were before them in the legal separation action, and end up spending more in attorney's fees than if they had just divorced in the first place. That being said, it's a great tool if both spouses are really trying to save their marriage.

INSIGHTS INTO A DIVORCE BETWEEN DOMESTIC PARTNERS

At the time of writing this chapter, Article 1 Section 29 in Utah was struck down, which had defined marriage as being between one man and one woman. Earlier in the week, another federal court judge struck down some of the polygamy laws here in Utah. Those two things, in essence, have changed the landscape completely in Utah concerning domestic partnerships and concerning gay and lesbian marriages.

From a legal standpoint, I think that the one interesting thing that will come out of this is that there will no longer be any perceived gender bias. I say that because I believe people often think, "Because she is the mom, she's going to get custody," or, "Because he's the dad, he's the one who's going to get minimum standard time." Now we will either have two moms or two dads coming before the court in a divorce action. It will be interesting to see how the law changes, develops, or progresses in these cases.

No longer will there be the argument in a custody battle that the mother is a better caretaker of the children than the father. Now that you will be dealing with two mothers who are bringing up the child (whether through adoption or artificial insemination), the stereotype that the mother is the better caretaker of the child won't apply. There are some serious issues that the court will have to deal with in the near future. I think better child custody determination factors will also be developed, that will be more gender-neutral than the present ones.

I anticipate that there will be some good laws that come out of it and judges are going to have to take a hard look at the new issues as they arise. I'm hoping that, as these cases progress through the court system, they will lead to clearer laws. For example, it wasn't until recently that the law decreed that, under divorce actions, if you find that your spouse is cohabitating with someone, then you don't have to pay alimony.

The question became, "What if my spouse is now gay and living with another male?" Or, if she's a woman with another woman, and they're sexually active with each other, is that cohabitation? It is something that Utah has always struggled with, and it has been difficult to get the issue in front of the court to convince them that it was cohabitation. There should be some progress in this area of the law. Another factor that I think will change is that the courts will look more closely at the moral standards of each party. I think moral standards are changing and whether you agree with them or not doesn't matter. The court needs to define what the basis will be for moral standards.

As the law develops in regard to domestic partnerships, I think it will benefit all couples, because the law will become clearer, and it will progress in a way that will help people argue their cases more clearly. I think it will provide judges better standards to rely on as they make custody determinations.

LITIGATED DIVORCE VERSUS SETTLING OUTSIDE THE COURT SYSTEM

There are certain steps that you must take before you even get to a litigation aspect in Utah. Usually couples will go through temporary orders, and then they'll go to mediation (which is required in Utah) after they exchange financials. It's rule 26.1 in Utah that each party has to disclose what's called a financial declaration. This includes bank statements and all assets and liabilities. Basically, the court wants to give you the tools to try to settle your divorce without litigating it. It wants you to go to mediation with the tools you need to settle your case in a manner that everyone can live with. The fact is, no one ever ends up completely happy after a divorce, because it always involves compromise.

If you don't settle in mediation, you are now moving towards trial and litigation of the issues, and there are a lot of costly things to be done in your case; for example, formal discovery. In formal discovery, there are interrogatories, requests for documents, and requests for admissions. They are written up by your attorney and sent off to opposing counsel. They have 30 days to respond to those, and you get the response back in writing. Many times, these documents just bring up more questions, so then your attorney takes depositions. You can get depositions from any party. For example, if there are child custody evaluators, you will want to get a deposition from the child custody evaluator of the other parent. You will want to get a deposition from any witnesses you plan on having in your trial.

As you can imagine, it becomes quite expensive very quickly to go through discovery and move towards trial. Once your case goes to trial, it can last one day or one week. It just depends on how many experts or evaluators there are. For example, we had a trial once which was quite long because it included a personality expert, three children's therapists, a child custody evaluator, a computer forensics expert, and police officers, all of whom were called as witnesses. How long your trial lasts, also may depend on what you are fighting about.

When it comes to custody, most parents feel that there is no price tag on their children, or on having time with them. Therefore, people are usually willing to spend whatever it takes to get the result they want. Sometimes that can be very expensive, and as you move forward through the litigation, it can be just as complicated as any other kind of civil litigation case, because it's under the same types of laws and identical rules of evidence and experts.

This is not something that you can do on your own. You definitely need an attorney to help you through your divorce, because there's a lot at stake. A good attorney can help you avoid simple mistakes that could really hurt your case. For example, we once had a case where opposing counsel had done a psychological sexual evaluation, and we fought for weeks about releasing that psychosexual evaluation in the divorce case. It took a court hearing just to deal with that one issue, but it was important because it influenced custody. Going through those steps mentioned throughout this chapter and making sure that you have all the appropriate evidence to put in front of the judge at the proper time is critical to your case.

The worst scenario is going to trial with this great piece of evidence that proves you are the better parent, and that you're better serving the best interests of the children, and having the judge tell you, "You can't introduce that evidence because you did not include it on your exhibit list." One little oversight like this can cost you the parenting schedule that you want.

It's important if you're going to litigate your case that you are properly prepared for trial, and that you hire an attorney who can successfully litigate your case. Interview a lot of attorneys. Interview until you find someone you trust and with whom you are comfortable, and who you feel can present your case in a very clear manner to help you get a great result. It takes time to find someone like that. He may be the first attorney you call, but you won't know until you talk to a couple of others. It's worth the effort of interviewing more than one attorney, because you're hiring someone who's going to affect the rest of your life.

INSIGHTS INTO HIGH ASSET DIVORCE CASES

High net-worth cases are complex divorces, usually involving a self-owned business that was started either during the marriage or before the marriage. The key to success in these cases is to hire a credible financial expert. If your case is going to trial, you need an expert upon whom the judge can rely. It's important to understand that your lawyer speaks for you, so what your lawyer says is not automatically going to be taken as unbiased truth.

Your attorney should know which experts to hire to examine specific issues. It's not a situation where you can simply look at tax returns, or look at pay stubs, and comprehend what a business is worth.

For example, if a self-owned business gets K1's at the end of the year, they can manipulate those K1's; so you need a CPA who can really look into the books for the information to support your valuation of the business. If you're going through the discovery process, your lawyer needs to talk to a CPA who can guide him in uncovering the real financial worth of the business. There are so many ways a business owner can legally manipulate the financial statements for tax purposes that, when taken at face value, they don't present an accurate picture of the business's worth. You would hate to miss out on something from a business valued at $20 million, because you believed the other side when they stated in mediation that it was worth $10 million. You want your divorce done quickly but not so quickly that you lose out on money that is due you.

It is imperative that you do your own evaluation, so you know exactly what you are negotiating about, and you understand the legal arguments that can be made. We encounter clients who may have a house in Arizona, a house in Utah, and a house in Colorado. We need to know when they were bought, how much money was put down, and where the money came from. Those questions alone are very important when figuring out how to divide these properties or deciding if and when they should be sold. Should they be sold immediately or maybe five years down the line? You need experts to help you make educated decisions. We see too many instances where people didn't use due diligence, and afterwards, they want to hire us to fix things, when it should have been done right the first time.

We have developed a checklist to review with the experts to hone in on the issues that are really important to the case. I can't tell you how many divorces I've negotiated where a party didn't even know that the other spouse had a bank account in another bank until going through our process. We went through the couple's bank statements and uncovered that there was another bank account. There was one divorce where we went through two years of bank statements on the husband and uncovered some weird transfers. That led to another subpoena where we discovered that the husband was funneling money through the business to his girlfriend. Had we missed that, my client would have lost out on her share of a large sum, unbeknownst to her.

When it comes to business, stocks, and investments, these all need to be valued correctly, because they will affect alimony and child support. Once you start getting into the upper echelon of income, meaning people in your state in the top 3% financially, then you are dealing with different child support issues than the other 97% of the population. That's where a good attorney who has experience with these issues can give you invaluable advice and make a difference in the outcome.

FAILURE TO DISCLOSE AN ASSET

In a high asset divorce case, another issue comes up if one party doesn't disclose everything and tries to hide an asset. Some changes have been made recently in Utah, whereby if you don't disclose an asset, any financial asset, then the other party potentially can be awarded the whole thing. For example, if a client didn't tell me about an account worth $10,000 cash, and somehow the other side found out, the other attorney could bring a motion in front of the court and say, "They didn't disclose it; therefore, that full $10,000 should be given to my client." I always tell my clients upfront, "I'd rather know about it and try to protect it than be in front of the court trying to say why you did not disclose something, and then run the risk of you losing it all."

In one case, we learned that the other party had been taking cash and putting it in a safe in the house, and he had not disclosed that in his financial declaration. When they discovered that we knew about this hidden asset, they were quick to try to settle and give my client half. We're going after all of it. The court has to punish parties who try to hide assets, because otherwise, they're encouraging this behavior and creating more problems for themselves. For instance, if I found out about a non-disclosed asset later in the divorce, technically, I could make a motion before the court to set the whole divorce aside, based on the other party not disclosing an asset and for their fraud. This would lead to a situation where more divorce cases would be going to trial, rather than being settled in mediation.

INSIGHTS INTO FATHER'S RIGHTS

Father's rights in Utah is a big movement. I think because of the state we're in, there's a preconceived notion that all fathers are at a disadvantage in their divorce actions. A common issue that fathers face is how much time they spent with their children compared to the mother, and what kind of parents they were. For instance, if the father was the parent who contributed the most financially to the marriage, and the mother was a stay-at-home mom, then the father is almost punished for that. In essence, the laws in Utah say they're gender neutral, but I think there are some legitimate issues that fathers face, and one is convincing the court that they can work full time (and the same goes for a mother who works full time), but also be the primary caretaker for the children.

Getting enough parenting time may seem like a father's rights issue, but often, it is just a question of schedules, and when the father is available to spend time with the children. I've heard many judges say that a relationship with both parents is best for the children, and many child custody evaluators feel the same. The most important thing that fathers can do to show they are good parents is to be active in their children's lives and demonstrate that they have a history of doing that; for example, going to parent–teacher conferences, coaching their children in their extracurricular activities, or helping with their homework. Many fathers who come to us are very active in the children's lives, and they get great results because they show the court that the children do benefit from a positive relationship with both parents.

One fact that the father just has to accept is that if he was the primary financial provider for the family, he will pay child support. It's just the normal course of business, and it's something that will benefit the children. But at the same time, the more parenting time he gets, the less child support he is going to pay. To get more parenting time, it's critical that the father is able to demonstrate to the court how active he has been in the children's life.

ISSUES INVOLVED WITH RELOCATION

Relocation commonly occurs after a party is divorced, and in the state of Utah, it covers cases where a parent moves 150 miles away or more. If a parent wants to move that far away, he or she must provide written notice to the other parent 60 days in advance. That's when the fireworks go off. That's when the other parent usually files one of two things: a petition to modify parenting schedule or a temporary restraining order to try to stop the parent from moving.

These cases become hotly contested very quickly. Many people call me and say, "I'm looking to move 200 miles away, what are my chances of keeping custody or changing custody?" If both parents are highly active in the children's lives, in Utah it can be very difficult to move more than 150 miles away and still keep custody of your children. The court believes that the children will benefit from both parents being in their lives on a consistent basis.

Most of the time, you'll be able to move if you were awarded sole physical custody. If you have sole physical custody and the other parent is just exercising minimum time with the children, you have a better chance of getting the court to agree. If you have 50/50 custody and parenting time with the children, it's going to be a lot harder. It's almost like doing your divorce all over again.

If a petition to modify is filed to try to stop you from moving, then you are going through a divorce action all over again. All the same issues need to be addressed in front of the court once again. The outcome is hard to predict. Most of the time, the relocation revolves around a job change or a new marriage; those types of things. Although these are legitimate issues, a petition to modify is still a very hard thing to get, especially if a child custody evaluation shows that the children benefit from interaction with both parents.

The courts will not tell you that you can't relocate, but they will say you can't move with your children. They will say that the children must stay here with the other parent. The parent subsequently decides not to move, and nothing changes in the child custody or parenting schedule. In the end, both parties will have gone through a lot of money in attorney's fees, and a lot of time and stress, and nothing will have changed.

There are some parents who still move, and they switch custody. Nevertheless, it's very highly-contested. The court can restrict the children from moving, because the court is looking out for the best interest of the children. Unfortunately, we've invited the court into our lives to decide what is right or wrong for the children.

INSIGHTS INTO PARENTAL ABDUCTION

In 1980, Congress enacted the Parental Kidnapping Prevention Act, or PKPA, as some family law attorneys call it. Its purpose was to protect children through custody orders that have been decided in other states, unless that state has declined the client's jurisdiction and the new state has extricated. For example, we've discussed parental relocation, but what happens in a situation where a mom gets up and leaves and takes the children to another state? Congress wanted to try to prevent that situation with the Parental Kidnapping Prevention Act. In effect, Congress is saying that states must enforce custody orders that were made in other states.

For example, if that mother flees to Arizona from Utah, Arizona has no power to change custody orders that were made in Utah. Let's say the mother tries to file a protective order in Arizona. The court in Arizona is going to look at the custody orders in Utah and, most likely, will return those children to Utah. A judge in Arizona will get on the phone with the judge in Utah who handled the divorce action, and say, "Are you declining jurisdiction or are you going to keep it up there?" Most of the time, the judge in Utah will say, "We're going to keep it up here because this is where the children are from, and it looks like the mom is fleeing." Under that act, Arizona has to bring the children and the mother back to Utah. If they don't come back, the court in Utah could actually issue a bench warrant for the mother's arrest.

Under the Parental Kidnapping Prevention Act, if a party flees just to try to keep the children away from the other spouse, there are going to be repercussions in the original state. Sometimes, if a party feels like he or she is losing the case, he or she will flee and think that he or she can just run away from the problem. For a state to have jurisdiction over a custody situation with the children, the children have to reside there for six months. That requirement doesn't make fleeing and staying for a week in a Motel 6 a sensible solution. Obviously, before you consider fleeing the state, you need to talk to an attorney and see if that action falls under the Parental Kidnapping Prevention Act.

If you were to flee the state, you would be susceptible to prosecution and/or jail time. It's a very serious situation and would not help your divorce case, because one of the considerations under the divorce action is determining which parent encourages a positive relationship between the children and the other parent. It's virtually like calling the judge and saying, "I'm not going to encourage a positive relationship with the other parent; I've fled the state, and I don't really want my children to see the other parent." If you have pending charges like that, it's seriously going to hinder your child custody situation in the divorce action. It's the same as committing an assault or domestic violence in front of the children. It is detrimental to children from the court's perspective.

INSIGHTS INTO CHILD CUSTODY

There are two types of custody: legal custody and physical custody. Legal custody in Utah refers to communicating with your ex-spouse about major things in your children's lives: for example, medical issues, school issues, and religious issues. The criterion for being granted joint physical custody in Utah, is having your children overnight for at least 30% of the year. That is important because it does tend to discourage relocation of the other spouse, and it also gives you more time with the children. Finally, the more overnights you have with your children, the lower your child support will be.

The statutes outline many factors for the court to consider when it comes to joint custody of the children. The first is whether the physical, psychological, and emotional needs and development of the children will benefit from a joint custody situation. The court will look at what has happened in the past concerning those things. This is one area where you may need experts to support your case.

The second consideration is the ability of the parents to give first priority to the welfare of the child or the children, and to make shared decisions that are in the best interests of the children. "First priority" are the key words that the judge will look for. Are you really putting your children first?

The third criterion that the court looks at is whether the respective parents are capable of encouraging and accepting a positive relationship between the child and the other parent. Are you talking negatively about the other parent in front of the children? Do you tell them their father is late on child support payment? What do you do to help encourage a positive relationship? Your children are already going through a hard time in their lives because of your divorce, so what are you doing to help improve that situation for them?

Another consideration is whether both parents participated in raising the child before the divorce. You need to be active in your child's life, and be able to prove it, if you want physical custody.

Next, the court will look at how close the parents live to each other. The closer you live to your ex-spouse, the more parent time you're going to get with the children. If you're granted primary physical custody of the children, and the other spouse lives nearby, then the court will try to give more time to that other parent, provided he or she is a good parent and fulfills all the other requirements of the court.

If the child is old enough (and the age in Utah seems to be 14), then the preference of the child can be taken into consideration. The court has to show that the child can form an intelligent preference as to the custody situation. Often, an attorney will make a motion for the judge to interview the child in chambers. The judge will take the child into chambers and assess the situation to determine if he/she has the maturity to declare a preference.

In addition, the maturity of the parents is looked at. Are you calling the police every time you want to go pick up your children? It doesn't show maturity if you can't communicate with your ex-spouse in a civil manner. They look at the past and the present to see if the parents have the ability to cooperate with each other and to make decisions jointly. This is a very difficult situation for most people because, obviously, things have broken down in the relationship to the point that they could no longer stay married.

Another factor the courts consider is the history of or potential for child abuse, spousal abuse, or kidnapping. When it comes to physical and legal custody, the court can consider any other factors that it deems relevant. There are some other things that child custody evaluators look at. One of the main ones is the ability to provide personal rather than surrogate care.

For example, it is always better that the children are with a parent than in daycare, so a parent who works all the time will be at a disadvantage. Another factor is significant impairment of the ability to function as parents; for example, if drug abuse or excessive drinking are involved.

Another interesting factor that is outlined, though little-used in Utah, is the religious compatibility with the child. Generally, this issue is only going to be raised in the case of a radical religion that would be considered a concern if the child participates.

A major consideration is the financial ability of a party to care for the children. If someone cannot hold down a job, or has a track record of not paying electric bills or other utilities, the court can take that into consideration when granting custody. Quite frankly, those are things that do address the best interest of the children. They are also things that responsible fathers can use to show that they can financially provide for their children.

CONTEMPT-OF-COURT ISSUES

Contempt in a divorce action occurs when somebody has violated the divorce decree order of the court. Your attorney would do what's called the "motion for an order to show cause," which is basically asking the party to appear before the court and tell the court why he or she should not be held in contempt for violating a divorce decree. The spouse who has violated the court order could be held in contempt and actually serve jail time and pay attorney's fees. Some common violations that occur are the denial of visitation and not paying child support or alimony.

The other day, there was a man before the court, who had not paid child support for eight months, and he was there for an order to show cause to be found in contempt. The judge found him in contempt and gave him seven days to pay the child support or he was going to do three days in jail. He was also ordered to pay the attorney's fees for the other side.

In essence, you're trying to enforce your divorce decree to hold the other party responsible for his obligations. If you get lazy and you don't do anything to force him to comply, the judge will look at your credibility. It's important that you stay up-to-date on those issues, and, coincidentally, they always seem to come up around the holidays. Non-compliance to the decree is something that the court does not take lightly, because they don't want you back in front of them. They want you to behave as adults and follow the divorce decree. Claiming that you cannot afford it is not a good enough excuse.

It's one of those situations where you better have a really good excuse, such as pending criminal charges or loss of a job. Even if you have lost your job, you need to file a petition to modify child support and get proactive on it before an order to show cause is brought before you. If you're found to be in contempt, those orders to show cause can be brought up later. If we petition the court to change custody or change parenting time, the court can look at you and say, "Well, you weren't a good parent by doing this (shirking your responsibility), so why shouldn't we take some parenting time away from you?"

It's a very serious situation, and it's not something to be taken lightly. You also need to enforce your divorce decree if those things are happening in your post-divorce case. Make sure you're protecting your interest as you move forward, because your divorce case is not really over until that last child is 18 and has graduated from high school. The issues will come up constantly, and you need to make sure you have a clear record before the court if you want the best results.

INSIGHTS INTO DOMESTIC VIOLENCE ISSUES

Domestic violence is a huge factor in the decision to award custody. Unfortunately, the courts do see a lot of domestic violence in divorce cases, but domestic violence is defined very differently from what the general public would understand. Yelling at your spouse in front of your children with a high threatening tone can be considered domestic violence in Utah. So you have to be really careful.

If you are the victim of domestic violence, you need to be proactive. You need to file for a protective order to protect yourself and your children and get that issue in front of the court. You need to remove yourself and your children from that highly-volatile situation. If domestic violence does occur, then you also need to call the police.

While some people falsify domestic violence, there are very real situations where it does occur. For those people, there are plenty of free services at the courthouse, especially in Utah. We have a free service for anyone seeking a protective order, to help you fill out the paperwork correctly, get it in front of the judge to get it signed that day, and actually serve it on your spouse for you. You shouldn't hesitate to utilize the services available to help you get the protection you need.

If you've been charged with domestic violence, and it did not occur, then you need to get proper representation from your divorce attorney and/or a criminal defense attorney. Whether or not violence actually occurred, it will affect your divorce case, especially if your spouse files for a protective order against you. You need to hire an attorney, but do not contact your spouse after you've been served. If you contact your spouse in any way, including using a third party to contact your spouse, it can be a class "A" misdemeanor; and if you do it again, it can be a felony. Actually, people have gone to jail for over a year for violating protective orders by just calling their spouse. You need to be careful and obey the law.

(This content should be used for informational purposes only. It does not create an attorney-client relationship with any reader and should not be construed as legal advice. If you need legal advice, please contact an attorney in your community who can assess the specifics of your situation.)

Donna J. Smiedt
Donna J. Smiedt
Arlington, TX

Donna Smiedt is a leading family law attorney in the Arlington-Dallas-Ft.Worth area. She combines approachable, sensitive counseling with aggressive and purposeful advocacy, delivering consistently successful legal representation for her clients. She offers hands-on case management to every client. This in-depth, personalized service allows her to get to the root of her client's concerns and anticipate and counter obstacles in the way of achieving her client's goals.

THE RESTRAINING ORDER

If someone is thinking about getting a divorce, I think being well-informed and prepared is the most important thing they can do for themselves. For most people, this time of their life is fraught with emotion. They're losing a sense of themselves and their self-worth. They are constantly thinking, "This person doesn't want me anymore, I must not have any value." Emotion clouds their judgment, when they really need to get prepared and look at their divorce as a dissolution of a business partnership. They need to think ahead, and ask themselves, "How could this other person hurt me financially if I don't take preventive steps immediately?"

The very first thing to do is to talk to an attorney and discuss your assets. I always advise that parties need to be cognizant of their rights in regard to joint bank accounts. In regard to joint accounts, there is always the concern that the other party could liquidate the joint account, leaving the other spouse with no access to funds for living expenses or attorney's fees. I advise my clients to transfer at least half of the funds into a joint account in my client's name solely just so that they are equally in control of community funds. It is very important to think ahead and be prepared, and take some type of action to minimize the damage that you could have financially.

It's also important to get a restraining order to stop the other party from spending money on anything that isn't necessary for ordinary and necessary living and business expenses. This Restraining Order prohibits the other spouse from spending or incurring debts on new items, withdrawing money from 401ks or IRAs as well as from incurring certain liabilities that may impact the other party. It's very important to look at the entire financial picture and put in place certain restrictions on spending and transferring assets to preserve the community estate.

Many lay people confuse a "protective order", which is usually what we obtain in the case of family violence situations, with a "restraining order." Restraining orders are common in Texas and in our Texas Family Code there are specific provisions authorizing the granting of a Temporary Restraining Order which merely serves to preserve the status quo in regard to the community estate and the status of the children of the marriage and prohibit certain actions by the spouses to stalk, intimidate or harass the other spouse merely because they are emotionally impacted by the actual filing of a divorce. The statute makes it easy to obtain a restraining order. You can send a runner up to the court house and the Texas Family Code provides that one may a obtain a restraining order against the property, against persons and children without having to actually file an affidavit, unless you're asking for extraordinary relief in regards to the children, or you're asking for what we call a "kick-out" order. A kick-out order is exactly what it sounds like; it kicks the person committing family violence out of the residence. Only if there's been family violence committed within the last 30 days in that restraining order, can you exclude another spouse from the marital residence, or exclude the child of the marriage from the other spouse.

The restraining order is an initial order that your attorney can obtain without having to appear in court and have a hearing. It's just a matter of filing and asking for it, and having it issued. The Family Code states that it will be issued without the necessity of a hearing, without the necessity of any evidence being given, or any affidavits, so it's pretty standard.

In that restraining order, there's language specifying that the parties are prohibited from spending any money in excess of what's necessary for normal, reasonable living expenses, attorney's fees, and business expenses. There is also a restraining order that prohibits any of the spouses from removing the personal property from the home. You don't want that other spouse backing the U-Haul up to the front door and taking all the furniture, because it's very expensive to get that furniture back. Unless you obtain a restraining order, anybody can go get their stuff at any time and move it to some other location. Without one, you find yourself paying your lawyer an exorbitant hourly amount to fight over the furniture.

Under the order, both parties will be prohibited from cutting off credit cards from the other spouse, changing the beneficiary on life insurance policies or IRAs. These orders are very simple to obtain in Texas. By using this order properly, nobody can get an upper hand and put the other spouse in a bad financial situation.

INSIGHTS INTO MARITAL DEBT

Debt's an interesting entity because in Texas, there really is no such thing as community debt. Nevertheless, people need to understand that credit is contractual. The relationship between a creditor and a debtor, for example, yourself and Visa or MasterCard, is primarily between you and that separate entity, and the family court does not have much power in the matter.

When people enter into a contractual relationship with a creditor, i.e., the Visa application arrives in the mail and they both sign it, they're actually jointly and severally liable. So if one of the spouses charges up $30,000 they are both responsible for the debt. That means, if the other side doesn't pay, you owe the entire amount. If one of the parties were to run up all the credit cards, it would put the other spouse in a difficult situation.

I sometimes advise my clients, if the wife has no money, to charge her attorney fees on the joint credit card, because his name's on it, and he becomes responsible for the debt. If a woman has been a stay-at-home mom and is starting out without a good job, then she's not going to have much credit, and we don't want her starting out burdened with a large amount of debt from attorney's fees. So if she has a choice of credit cards, she should use a joint one.

Sometimes in a divorce, attorney fees don't get equalized. So, I do advise clients: If you have a joint credit card that you're authorized to use, put the necessities on there, such as attorney fees or apartment rent, because that will make the other party be responsible.

Obtaining a restraining order basically keeps the *status quo*, and it avoids compromising your property settlement later, or your property division by the court. In Texas, you can use the same restraining order, to apply to the parties' behavior. Unfortunately, human nature is such that oftentimes, especially in the beginning of a divorce, and more often with younger couples, a spouse may be calling repeatedly at work, yelling and screaming and cussing at the other spouse who's leaving the marriage. They may be calling at all hours of the night, using profane or obscene language, embarrassing them and just being plain ugly. This behavior does not rise to the level of domestic violence, but we want to prophylactically stop that from happening.

So we obtain the restraining order, and you're in contempt of court if you then send 50 text messages using profane language, or call them at work. It's stressful, and it can affect the person's job to have somebody harassing them. When the order gets puts in place, it's not excluding somebody from the house, and it doesn't say that they can't talk to that spouse, but they cannot talk to them in ugly, demeaning language. It's saying you need to behave while this case is pending, and it's an easy fix to stop harassment. The third part of the general restraining order that's authorized by the Family Code, and is obtainable without a hearing or an affidavit, deals with the children.

Another very important provision in the restraining order prevents the parent whom the restraining order is being served from withdrawing the children from school, changing the residence of the children, and removing the children from the jurisdiction of the court for purposes of changing the residence. It stops that parent from saying, "Okay. I'm getting a divorce and I'm going to back up the U-Haul truck and get all my stuff, and now I'm going to drive to Alaska where my parents live and hang out there with the kids. I'm going to pull them out of school and re-enroll them in a school in Alaska." Without the restraining order, my client could be left in the difficult position of trying to get his or her children back.

Judges want the children kept in the *status quo* so that the children are not completely torn apart. They're already going to be upset by the whole concept of divorce, and mom and dad not living together in the house. They don't need to be ripped out of school and moved to a completely new community without any court oversight.

In every divorce there is the issue of dividing property, whether that means a retirement plan, a family business, or a huge estate. Even so, there are going to be issues that only apply to that specific client. For instance, is the house in both their names? You need the help of an experienced attorney to deal with the special issues that apply to your unique circumstances.

You might have a situation where you obtained a house and it's not in both of your names. The party with the title could sell that piece of property if it's in his or her name alone. As a divorce attorney, I always ask my client if they've been to counseling. Some people rush into divorce and I always inquire if counseling might help. Actually, Texas has a counseling statute, wherein if either party files for counseling, the court could order the parties to go to counseling.

INSIGHTS INTO CHILD CUSTODY

Custody is very complex and it's very fact-specific issue in a divorce. In Texas, if you don't have children, you can just file a divorce and be done with it. If you have children, it's automatically going to be classified as a "suit affecting parent-child relationship", and even if you aren't married and you have children together, you would be involved in a suit affecting parent-child relationship that lawyers call a SAPCR.

There can also be grandparent issues. Sometimes grandparents want custody and that would fall under SAPCR. So a "suit affecting parent-child relationship" is anything regarding the children. The facts in each case are very relevant, even the way a person behaves in pre-filing is relevant.

It's important to strategize and plan ahead. I wouldn't advise you to be the parent who tries to move the child to Alaska in my previous example, because the judges are going to say, "Maybe that person doesn't have the best interest of the children at heart." That would earn a black mark against you. Women who don't have their own income and maybe have been stay-at-home moms often think, "Oh, my God, my husband said he's not going to pay me a dime and if I leave him, we're going to be left without anything." Their fears are unfounded, because in Texas, you have a legal duty to support your spouse. If you're the main wage-earner and the other party has stayed at home, you will have to pay temporary spousal support as well as temporary child support in order to maintain the non-working spouse.

What happens while your divorce is going through the legal process is dependent on the facts of your case and how much money comprises the community estate. Obviously, if the person who's working earns a good wage and can pay child support and pay for the house, and keep that homemaker in the house with the kids, the judge is going to order that maintained until we get past the initial stages of the divorce. Unless that homemaker/spouse has issues such as alcoholism, drugs, or a history of mental problems, the judge is most likely going to keep that person in the home with the kids, and they're going to make the other person move out.

It's not because they want to penalize the person who's working, but it's because the court has to look out for the best interest of the children. As said earlier, the best interest of the children is often to keep them in the status quo; to keep them in the home that they're used to, keep them going to the same school, and keep them going to the same church camp or summer camp. The children's lives should be changed as little as necessary, because they'll already be going through a hard time coping with the divorce.

If a mother leaves the kids and takes off to Florida with her boyfriend, then it's going to hurt her custody case if she doesn't come back for six months, that's enough to lose the edge on custody. The manner in which parties deal with outside relationships is very important a custody case. If somebody chooses a paramour over a spouse, or commits bad acts regarding that paramour in front of the children, these things are more significant than most people think. Part of my responsibility to my clients is to make sure they understand that certain behaviors in outside relationships are unacceptable to the court.

For example, there is no acceptable recreational drug use when you're in a custody case. Your entire life is under a magnifying glass and you cannot make a mistake. While you're planning to get divorced and in the middle of a custody case, you absolutely have to make sure that your lifestyle could survive scrutiny.

If you're a homemaker and you've been doing drugs, you want it out of your system before you go to court. There's a lot of planning involved with that, too. You don't want to be staying out every night partying with your friends, or spending the night with your paramour and leaving your other spouse home to take care of your children, if you want custody.

RESTRAINING ORDERS TO MANIPULATE CHILD CUSTODY

I caution a client that seeking a domestic violence restraining order strictly as a way to manipulate custody is a double-edged sword. I think it's extremely unethical for any lawyer to be a part of that. Unless they actually have proof of violence to back up their claim, I will instruct them not to seek the order, unless I'm genuinely concerned about a client's safety.

Client safety is very important to me. I had a client who was killed by her spouse while they were going through divorce. That was a horrible experience, and I acknowledge that divorces can push people over the edge. If there is any real concern about family violence, you need to be super vigilant. Having said that, there's no piece of paper, as was proven by my client's death two years ago, that's going to keep you safe. If you feel unsafe and you cannot legally obtain that type of protective order, you need to go into hiding.

You will need to go somewhere until it's safe, because you're a sitting duck at the house and if the other spouse really wants to hurt or kill you, a piece of paper is not going to stop him. Usually, if you are concerned about your safety, your attorney will obtain an *ex parte* order. Such orders can be hard to obtain, but a good lawyer can figure out what to insert into the affidavit. The affidavit goes into detail about how the party was abused. For instance, it may detail how he choked her on this day, or threw her to the ground while she was pregnant, or kicked her in the stomach.

All of the acts of family violence should be set forth in the affidavit. Then the judge reviews the affidavit and if they believe that there is an imminent danger to the spouse that warrants the issuance of the order without first having a hearing, the judge will sign the Ex Parte Protective Order. Then a hearing will be scheduled for within 14 days where you're required to present the evidence to back up the request for the order.

Sometimes, a client tells me, "He did all of this. He's been terrible. He strangled me. He hit me in the stomach," and I say, "Did you call the police?" "No." "Did you go to the hospital or a doctor?" "No." "Did you take any pictures of the abuse?" "No." At that point, a red flag goes up. A seasoned lawyer on the other side is going to say "Well, they can't prove any of that." Then the judge is going to look closely at the person that would actually do this to her children, deprive them of access to the other parent, and make up something like that which could affect this other parent's life and the lives of the children forever. That's very close to what we call "parental alienation." As you can see, a dishonestly-obtained restraining order can back-fire horribly.

There's a fine line to walk as a family attorney. You must discern if your client's in danger, and truly has been abused, or is trying to use that accusation to get a leg up on their spouse. The latter is just not acceptable. It's not good for the children, and I would never be a part of that. There are some people who don't call the police, who stay in that relationship, but most of them who are beaten up and have had black eyes have friends who have noticed. If somebody has been beaten up and has gone to the hospital, and has two black eyes, a broken nose and a broken jaw, then that person needs a protective order.

INSIGHTS INTO PARENT ALIENATION ISSUES

Parent alienation is an interesting subject and it's a very difficult case for the lawyers. If you have any type of alienation occurring in your relationship with your children, it's important that you obtain a really good family law attorney who has the knowledge and is experienced enough to recognize this scenario. It's extremely difficult to prove, because most of the time it's done behind closed doors with the child. It often begins with a parent saying things like, "Daddy hits me. Daddy just abused me. Daddy doesn't love me anymore. Daddy doesn't like you. He's leaving us. Daddy said he never wanted to have children in the first place. Daddy wanted Mommy to have an abortion." The mother has started to tell the child horrible, terrible things about that other parent, and it's all done behind closed doors.

You obtain a protective order, and you keep Dad away, and you say "Dad's terrible," or even worse, you make allegations of sexual abuse.

The other parent's lawyer is telling him, "Well, I don't want you to be alone with the child because you don't want to get arrested for any kind of sexual misconduct with your child. Therefore, you need to step back. It can actually end with the child not having a relationship with that particular parent. And unfortunately, there are parents out there who are vindictive enough to do that to their own child because they hate the other parent so much.

When a case comes into my office, I tell my clients, "You have to love your child more than you hate your spouse," because it does the child no good to grow up thinking that one-half of them, the other parent, is this horrible, disgusting person. Unless your spouse has committed child abuse and spousal abuse, don't taint the children's opinion of their other parent, because it only creates psychological problems for the children as they grow up.

The person who's being alienated needs to have a good lawyer who will ask that the child see a counselor and that the situation be looked into immediately. A social study can be initiated to look into the circumstances of both parents in the home, and the children can be interviewed frequently by somebody who can discern when a child is being coached to say something. Some children are just pleasers, or for certain psychological reasons, they are easily manipulated by one parent because they want to make that parent happy. Unless the child is truly being abused, and needs to be protected, you really have to watch out for alienation, because it's a ghastly thing.

If a child protective services case ensues, it might be weeks before the accused parent can see the child, and it may be only in a supervised environment. Keeping a child and parent apart is absolutely horrific for both the child and the parent if there really is no wrongdoing. Those are the most difficult cases, and both sides require a highly-skilled family law practitioner to intervene in these cases. The best interest of the child is not being served, because no child is helped by severing the relationship with one of his or her parents just because the parents are getting a divorce, unless there's actually been that type of abuse.

INSIGHTS INTO COLLABORATIVE LAW

Collaborative law is a new vehicle that is available under the Texas Family Code. It is available for parties obtaining a divorce, and also for suits affecting the parent-child relationship. Collaborative law is a form of alternate dispute resolution or what we call ADR, which includes mediation, arbitration, and now collaboration. The whole idea behind collaborative is to avoid litigation, where you have attorneys arguing your case and the court deciding the fate of your entire family. Both parties and the professional team sign an agreement stating that they will not go to court in this case.

The idea behind the collaborative process is that both lawyers and both clients reach a settlement together. Essentially, you're handing the reins over to the interested parties, the husband and wife, to settle their differences in regard to the business, the property division, and most importantly, how they're going to parent their children, and how they're going to pay child or spousal support. In litigation, you may go into a court room and wait for hours behind 10 other people to talk to the judge, with your lawyer billing you for all that time that you're sitting there waiting. Even then, the judge might not reach you, and may tell you to go to lunch and come back. So you're getting billed for eight hours, while the lawyer ultimately spends 15 minutes in front of the judge, trying to get relief for you. In collaborative law, we schedule meetings ahead of time with both parties. This translates to tremendous savings.

In Texas, we utilize the full collaborative group, which includes a mental health professional as a neutral party, and a financial professional as a neutral party. So the collaborative group is comprised of two lawyers, one representing each of the clients, and two neutrals (a financial neutral and a mental health professional neutral). Maybe you don't need a mental health professional in case, but the mental health professional is actually what we call the communications facilitator. He or she facilitates and runs the meetings, and makes sure we follow the correct procedures.

All parties, including the attorneys, sign an agreement before we start this process, where we agree that we're all going to do this collaboratively, and that we're not going to lie to each other. We're going to produce documents that are requested. It's very transparent, and nobody is going to hide anything. Basically, we're an open book, and we're sharing everything. The mental health professional presides over the meeting, and makes sure we stick to the agenda. We strive to be kind and respectful to each other. The entire process is confidential and the details of the meeting may not be disclosed by any of the parties or the professional team.

The ultimate goal is that we use interest based negotiation, which is a very well-known formula for resolving conflict. Everybody has an interest, and instead of focusing on beating each other up and using all the negatives we know about each other, like we do in litigation, we try to look at what the other party is interested in. Maybe they want a parenting schedule that the judge isn't likely to give them, because they have a weird work schedule, and both parties have to co-operate with each other to work around it.

Hopefully, we're also teaching our clients some valuable skills in these meetings, because we are skilled negotiators. We've gone through courses and we've been collaboratively-trained. Most clients lack this skill, and they're going to have to deal with each other until the last child is 18, or until they're walking down the aisle with them when the kid's 22 and getting married. They'll have to talk about who's paying for what in the wedding. You don't want your parents yelling and screaming at each other at the church. So we're giving them tools to help them co-parent and resolve conflicts with this type of negotiation.

The best reward is to hear clients say, "You taught me how to deal with my ex-husband, so now we have a good co-parenting relationship. We don't have to run back to court every time we can't agree on where the child's going to school, or if we're keeping the child back one year." All of these decisions should be made by parents, not by judges. That's the whole idea behind collaborative law: that you're maximizing your time with your attorney, and then your attorney becomes a settlement advisor, as opposed to a hired gun.

Another good thing about collaboration is that it's very private. We all agree that everything will be kept confidential. People with large estates might have some issues that they don't want being made public. Every marriage has things that need not become public knowledge. Maybe a business owner doesn't want his employees at the factory to know about their boss. Especially if you have a large-asset case, collaborative law really pays off because you're not exposing all of your private financial dealings or your personal shortcomings in a public court room.

I think one of the most important things with collaborative law, is that you have a seasoned lawyer, who can look at the parties and get an idea of what their relationship is, what the personalities are, and whether there are mental health issues with one of the parties. He or she should be able to assess the case to determine whether or not this particular case is a good fit for collaborative. If the parties don't have the right personalities, if you don't pick the right lawyers, if you don't pick a financial professional who can work well with the two lawyers and the mental health professional, then you're not going to have a good result. If you don't have somebody that you can trust, you could have a disastrous outcome. I practice in a collaborative group with like-minded lawyers who I have known for 30 years, and they have the same attitude towards the resolution of cases that I do. They're ethical. We're using collaborative law so that we can have the best possible outcome for our clients. I would never go into a collaborative case with a non-collaboratively-trained lawyer. It's just that if I'm wrong about the attorney on the other side, then it could have a disastrous expensive outcome for my client.

It seems like everybody now has heard the catchword, 'collaborative' and they call you up and say, "I want a collaborative divorce and we've got a house and a 401k plan, and one kid, and a car that we share." For that case, it's not justified to have so many professionals that you're paying a lot of money, because that's a simple divorce case. They're not going to have enough assets to justify the expense.

Collaborative is appropriate for a complex property situation, where oftentimes there are issues regarding the evaluation of businesses. In litigation, we spend a lot of money on discovery, where we each hire our own forensic CPAs, and they come up with dueling evaluations of the business. You go to court hoping the judge picks yours, and the whole process can be extremely expensive.

With collaboration, we're going to pick a neutral party who is not trying to get the upper hand on anybody, and this person's going to evaluate the businesses. He meets with the client offline, and gathers all the information, and the case is an open book. This forensic CPA who the group has hired as the financial neutral assess and evaluates the estate and then assists in developing options to discuss with the team to divide the assets in the best way possible for both the clients.

The lawyers can effectively do their job as settlement advisors, instead of trying to be evaluation experts. We all work together, and it's really making good use of community funds to hire these experts because otherwise, you're doing double the work and spending twice as much money. Again, if you don't have a large estate, this expense is not justified because you have to pay two lawyers, a mental health professional, and a forensic CPA.

With a simple estate, if both agree on the appraisal of how much the house is worth, then a lawyer can sit down and put it all on a spreadsheet and figure it out, and only charge somebody for an uncontested divorce. In fact, they can both sit down with me, as long as the non-represented spouse realizes that he is not represented by me. He can take what was agreed to and go talk to his own lawyer for one session and pay him by the hour, and we can resolve this case. You don't need to have 10 meetings with all these professionals. There are other alternatives, and one is an uncontested divorce. The other is mediation.

If you go to a lawyer-mediator, then you can get the case settled, then go see another lawyer and just pay them to draft the documents in an uncontested divorce. So there are a lot of other options. Unless you have large custody issues or a large estate, I don't think collaborative is always the best route, because it's just not cost-effective.

HIGH-ASSET ESTATE AND COMPLEX PROPERTY DIVISION

Businesses make divorce cases more complicated, especially closely-held family businesses, because a lot of times, they provided a good income for the family, and you have an owner spouse running the business. Often, both spouses were running the business together, and dividing the work load. Maybe one was in sales, out there on the road, and the other was running the office, or maybe one was doing the bookkeeping, while the other was talking to the customers and running the staff.

Evaluation is difficult, because the value of a company is usually what somebody would pay for it. Many times we have to get creative about how we're going to divide that small closely-held family business. We want to keep it running, but still make sure that the spouse who's giving it up is going to receive adequate compensation for the salary they used to receive from it.

Another consideration is that you're not ultimately going to get paid the same as when you were running the business, where, for instance, maybe your car was paid for by the business. Generally speaking, if you have a very successful business, you will need a forensic valuation of the worth of the business, because it may be your largest asset and it needs to be divided correctly. Hopefully, you have enough other assets in the estate so that one of the parties can keep the business and the other spouse can receive other assets in exchange for his or her share in the business. It can get a little more complicated when the business has a buy-sell agreement, because the agreement may require one spouse to buy the other spouse's share of the business at a certain price. Oftentimes we have to utilize a secured payment to pay the other spouse out their share over time.

Many times with a closely held business, we have to figure out a way to raise capital in that business to buy out the other spouse. But again, you would need an experienced lawyer who can develop options with the business appraiser or the forensic CPA. It is unlikely that the spouse would want to continue to own shares in the business as a minority shareholder. If there were another partner, after the wife got her half share, she would no longer have a voice in the business. The other partner could decide to withhold distributions, and she would never get here share of the capital out of the business.

In the type of situation described above, you don't want to go see the judge. Those are really excellent cases for the collaborative process, because if we go into court, the judge might just say, "I'm going to order the sale of the business. I don't care what the business appraiser says. Whatever the market bears, that's the value." The result then is that both parties are stuck with having to negotiate with each other over the next 12 months' distributions. If you can work out an alternative solution to the court room, it is best for both parties. They can customize their own settlement, and reach a resolution that is acceptable to both parties.

INSIGHTS INTO PROFESSIONAL PEOPLE WITH HIGH INCOMES

You will need an experienced lawyer who can sit down with you in the beginning of your divorce and strategize how to divide assets if there is a professional business involved. The problem lies in the fact that professional businesses have very little value in the way of assets, and most of the value lies in goodwill. In a professional business, goodwill is attributed to the professional, i.e., the doctor, dentist, or lawyer. Lawyers are a very interesting example, because Texas law is clear that an attorney's goodwill is completely separate property which is not going to be divided with the spouse. Therefore, we know that goodwill exists, but we have to design an equitable work-around that fact when determining how marital assets are going to be divided.

Sometimes, you have practices where there's a great deal of this personal goodwill and also a lot of assets. Let's say that that dentist has five different locations, and he's hired young dentists to work for him, who are his employees. He has lots of equipment that needs to be updated, and old x-ray machines that cost a lot of money. If you have a lot of hard assets, all of those need to be taken into account and divided in the divorce.

They will typically value the practice at X amount and he has to pay it back over time out of his salary. Well, guess what? In Texas, it is a community property asset. The doctor paid $500,000 to join the practice. Therefore, his interest is at minimum worth $500,000. Knowing that the divorce lawyers are coming, they write their buy-and-sell agreements where they fix the price and the value of the practice so you must use that value in your divorce negotiations.

A lot of doctors now own their surgical buildings. Many years back, they only had privileges at a little hospital and they didn't own any part of the hospital. Surgical centers are viable, very profitable businesses. The scenario is that you get a group of eight doctors, who together own a surgical building, and they hire the surgical staff, the nurses, a manager, and they own the property.

That's a viable business in and of itself, outside of the goodwill of the doctor. If the doctor owns an interest in a surgical complex that's grossing $7 million a year and eight doctors own it, then we need to look at how to use this asset as part of our negotiations. These situations are very complex and you need an attorney with experience to navigate the roadblocks that are put into place to protect the doctor, and are to the detriment of the spouse.

CONCLUSION

I've been practicing for almost 30 years and I love it. I get to meet a lot of people and I feel as though I help them cope with a very difficult time in their lives. There are times when you see human nature at its worst. Unfortunately, when people go through a divorce and have a fear of losing their children, it becomes so personal and so emotional that it affects their judgment. That's why it's important to have a good lawyer who makes a client pay attention to the important things, not just how much money they're getting or how many more days they're getting with the child than their spouse, but what's in the best interest of the child.

I think I have an excellent reputation for being a very skilled litigator, and I've beaten a lot of people up in court. That's my job, and that's what a client pays me to do when I'm the litigator, but I really think lawyers and the public need to ask if this the best place to resolve your family disputes, because your children are going to be affected by this. The way Mom and Dad get along in the future is so important to their children's welfare. It is often possible to reach a resolution between the two of them, without hiring big guns to tear them apart in court, and having some stranger in a black robe, making the most important decisions of their life for them. I think everybody needs to think about how alternative dispute resolution forums, be they mediation or collaborative law, can give them back control and result in better outcomes than going directly into litigation.

(This content should be used for informational purposes only. It does not create an attorney-client relationship with any reader and should not be construed as legal advice. If you need legal advice, please contact an attorney in your community who can assess the specifics of your situation.)